BURRATA

BURRATA

A JOURNEY THROUGH CRAFT, FLAVOUR & TRADITION

This book is an homage to burrata cheese, an exquisite cheese introduced to Australia by Giorgio Linguanti.

In the last ten years, this queen of Italian cheeses has taken over the international cheese scene, holding a special place in everyone's hearts.

Burrata, meaning 'buttered' in Italian, is a fresh cheese that marries mozzarella and cream in perfect union. Its heart, the stracciatella (pronounced *stretch-yah-tella*), is a sumptuous blend of shredded mozzarella and cream, encased by a soft mozzarella shell. As the knife glides through the burrata, its creamy core oozes out, heralding a moment of pure delight.

This exquisite delicacy hails from Apulia, more commonly referred to by its Italian name, Puglia, a southern region in Italy. This lush region is a stronghold of cheesemaking, celebrated for its rich dairy farming heritage and the artistry of burrata making. In Puglia, renowned for its rolling hills, sheer cliffs, white medieval towns and endless century-old olive groves, burrata is more than a delicacy; it symbolises the artisanal skills passed down through generations.

This book will explore the intricate art of burrata cheesemaking and celebrate the passionate stories of the artisans who have dedicated their lives to this treasure, sharing over 60 recipes that highlight this delicacy, from entrees all the way to desserts.

Prepare to be inspired and delighted by the story of burrata, a cheese that embodies love, craftsmanship and the essence of Puglia.

RIGHT Giorgio Linguanti, owner of That's Amore Cheese, in Alberobello, Puglia

GIORGIO'S JOURNEY

13

FROM SICILY TO BURRATA MASTERY

Giorgio's tale begins not in the lush green pastures of a dairy farm, nor within the walls of a bustling cheese factory, but in the aisles of a supermarket in Sicily. A young university student disillusioned with academia, Giorgio found his calling amid the deli cheese section, where his fascination for the pungent aromas of gorgonzola and taleggio first sprouted.

'In Sicily, the distinctive mould essence of blue cheese was often greeted with turned-up noses,' Giorgio reflects. Contrary to popular taste, he found a unique allure in the more pungent, aromatic cheeses. Here, in this unassuming supermarket, Giorgio's lifelong romance with cheese began to take shape.

In the '90s, Sicily, a land rich in culinary traditions, had yet to be graced by the treasure of burrata cheese. This hidden gem was nestled in its birthplace, Puglia, awaiting its moment to captivate palates globally. There, in his Sicilian hometown, Giorgio was on the verge of an extraordinary journey that would intimately connect his destiny with the yet-to-be-revealed wonders of burrata.

In a charming shop nestled among the Aeolian Islands, Giorgio's venture, La Bella Aeoliana – 'the beautiful Aeolian' – came to life. The shelves were adorned with the islands' finest offerings: sweet Malvasia wines, capers grown under the warm sun, and tuna preserved in fine oil, a testament to Giorgio's passion for food.

A variety of antipasti beckoned locals and travellers alike, each item a reflection of Sicily's culinary heritage. After La Bella Aeoliana's third year, Giorgio embraced the spirit of adventure, making the bold decision to pursue a new and exciting venture in Australia, a multicultural canvas.

Upon arriving in Melbourne, Giorgio faced a myriad of challenges. The language barrier was daunting – he spoke little to no English, which made everyday interactions and securing employment a significant hurdle. He was in a foreign land with customs and traditions that were vastly different from those in his hometown. The buzzing streets of Melbourne were a stark contrast to the serene, sunlit landscapes of Sicily. Yet Giorgio was full of excitement and determination, ready to embrace his new life.

Despite having no prior cheesemaking experience, Giorgio secured a job in a cheese factory. Though the factory was worlds away from the artisanal cheesemaking practices he had witnessed in Sicily, Giorgio embraced the challenge with enthusiasm. He immersed himself in the craft, learning new techniques each day and developing an understanding of the Australian palate.

'I was brimming with the excitement of discovery and the pleasure of sharing my passion for one of the gastronomic world's finest treasures. In my quest for knowledge, I contacted my brother back in Sicily, asking him to send me books about cheese, especially those written in Italian,' Giorgio reminisces. The books his brother sent became Giorgio's lifeline, connecting him to his roots and providing him with a wealth of knowledge. His desire to master the art of hand-making cheese, which was not a common practice in Australia, led him to study these techniques and experiment meticulously.

Giorgio started making cheese at home, beginning with 'sfoglia di mozzarella', bocconcini leaf, which quickly became a favourite among friends. Word of his artisanal skills spread, and soon Giorgio was waking up early each morning to meet the increasing demand from local eateries.

A pivotal moment came when a customer sparked Giorgio's interest in burrata.

'Giorgio, do you make burrata?' the customer inquired. Filled with determination, Giorgio replied, 'Yes, I am starting soon!'

Having never seen burrata before, Giorgio was intrigued. 'When I moved to Australia in 2004, I had never seen burrata in Sicily. Initially, it was very regional, but then it started spreading to major cities like Milan, Rome, Bologna and New York. When a client requested it, I decided to learn how to make it. I researched online because I couldn't afford to go back to Italy, so I just taught myself.'

LEFT Polignano a Mare, Puglia

Researching and experimenting with various techniques, Giorgio undertook many trials to create burrata. His journey of exploration finally resulted in a refined burrata, tailored for fine dining. This quickly became a staple in Melbourne's leading restaurants. Burrata's popularity was spreading, and Giorgio was not surprised. As he puts it:

> **'Burrata is the sexiest cheese on the market** and presents beautifully, giving chefs a great hero ingredient to create something unique.'

Word of Giorgio's exceptional cheeses soon spread, and his humble business began to grow. As the demand increased, so did his team.

In 2008, Giorgio founded That's Amore Cheese, aptly named to signify 'That's Love'. The business was modest at first, but quickly gained a loyal customer base, including some of Melbourne's top restaurants. What began as a small operation evolved into a thriving company that processes 6 million litres of milk per year and employs 120 staff members.

Through his multi award-winning business, Giorgio honours the traditions of Italian cheesemaking, sharing his beloved passion with his loyal community. Giorgio's knowledge and passion has enriched this book, and his dedication and contribution to this beautiful art has made him a pivotal figure in the world of burrata.

RIGHT Burrata making at That's Amore Cheese, Melbourne

18 WHY BURRATA?

THE ALLURE OF CREAMY INDULGENCE

Burrata, which translates to 'buttered' in Italian, is not just a cheese, it's an experience; a combination of textures and flavours that transcends the ordinary. Its allure lies in its unique composition and the delightful contrast it offers.

Burrata is a harmonious blend of mozzarella and cream. A smooth, firm mozzarella casing holds creamy strips of mozzarella bathed in cream. This juxtaposition of textures is both surprising and deeply satisfying to the palate.

Imagine slicing into a perfectly crafted burrata. As your knife gently breaks through the soft mozzarella exterior, the creamy, luscious interior begins to ooze out, inviting you to indulge.

This sight alone is enough to make your mouth water, but the aroma truly captivates. The delicate scent of fresh milk and cream promises a rich and decadent experience.

Burrata's versatility only adds to its allure. Serve it simply with a drizzle of high-quality olive oil and a sprinkle of sea salt for an elegant appetiser that highlights the cheese's natural beauty. Pair it with ripe, juicy tomatoes and fragrant basil for a classic Caprese salad, melding the burrata with the sweet acidity of the tomatoes and the aromatic punch of the basil. Add it to a rustic pizza or a fresh pasta dish, elevating the meal to new heights.

Unlike other cheeses, burrata's flavour profile is subtle yet complex, meaning it pairs beautifully with various ingredients, from ripe fruits like figs and pears to robust vegetables such as roasted beets and artichokes.

GIOVANI COLTIVATORI
Extra Berry
TOP FRUIT sas

THE ROOTS OF RICHNESS

HISTORY OF BURRATA

THE ORIGINS AND EVOLUTION OF BURRATA CHEESE

Nearing the heart of Puglia, the landscape is dominated by olive trees, almond trees and majestic oaks. Nestled within this picturesque region is Andria, a place where time seems to slow down. The earthy aroma of freshly tilled soil mingles with the sweet scent of blossoming olive trees. In this serene setting, overlooking the Puglian flatlands and the Adriatic Sea, stands Castel del Monte. The castle has come to be seen as a symbol of the region's historical and cultural significance.

In the early twentieth century, within these sun-kissed landscapes, burrata emerged as a clever solution to minimise waste and maximise flavour. Cheese artisans sought to use the leftover scraps of mozzarella. They took these remnants, known as 'stracciatella' (pronounced *stretch-yah-tella*), meaning 'little shreds', and combined them with fresh cream, encasing the mixture in a smooth, pliable mozzarella shell.

Production was limited, making burrata a rare treat that encapsulated the richness of Italian dairy farming and the artisanal skills handed down through generations. The cheese's name, derived from the Italian word 'burro', meaning butter, hints at the creamy, indulgent experience it offers.

THE TALE OF TWO CREATORS

Burrata's origins are as rich and complex as the cheese itself, with two compelling stories vying for credit as its true inventor. Two dedicated masters have perfected the art of burrata: Francesco Asselta and Lorenzo Bianchini. Both men, deeply rooted in the heart of Andria, claim to have invented this creamy delicacy, each with a narrative that reflects the ingenuity and resourcefulness of their time.

Lorenzo Bianchini's story takes us back to the 1950s. As the legend goes, one particularly harsh winter day, heavy snowfall blocked the roads, leaving Lorenzo with an abundance of mozzarella he could not sell. Refusing to waste the valuable curds and cream, Lorenzo decided to create a new product. In a moment of ingenious creativity, he crafted a natural casing from mozzarella and filled it with mozzarella scraps and fresh cream. In that moment, burrata was born.

Lorenzo's method not only preserved the precious curds and cream, but also introduced a new, luxurious cheese that delighted the palates of many.

The Asselta family tale is equally compelling. Around the same time, Francesco Asselta, also eager to maximise the use of dairy products, developed his own method of crafting burrata.

LEFT Castel del Monte, built in the 13th Century by King Frederick II

'My uncle Francesco was always playing around with cheese, forming it into shapes of little animals for the kids, like little horses, pigs and doves. He never saw cheese as a static food but rather as a joy to be delighted by,' reminisces Antonio.

'Francesco was playing with the curd and decided to experiment. One day he said, "Oh, I can put something inside." He made the first burrata, filling it with ricotta,' his nephew Antonio recounts with a smile.

Antonio describes the delicate technique: 'You took a piece of mozzarella, made a hole, and blew into it to inflate it, making the pouch. It was quite a skilful process.'

This blend of innovation and craftsmanship marked the birth of burrata, a cheese that would soon captivate the hearts and palates of many.

Antonio's narration reveals a fascinating glimpse into the cheese's evolution. The transition from using ricotta to stracciatella was another step in the cheese's development. 'My uncle Francesco was always experimenting. He started using cream when electricity allowed them to separate it,' Antonio explains.

Antonio notes, 'In the early days, the method of sealing burrata varied. We sealed the head by warming the mozzarella with hot water and squeezing it closed. Some people made knots; some people sealed them in diverse ways. Everyone started to differentiate their methods.'

As time progressed and technology advanced, methods continued to evolve. 'Packaging burrata was an intricate process. The cheese was wrapped in "carta pergamenata", an old Italian baking paper, and packed in leaves to sell, which helped cover some costs. However, as new producers entered the market, they started using nets instead of pine leaves. Eventually, we also stopped the traditional wrapping method. It was a big job because when you pull them out from the ground, they have a bulb that needs to be trimmed and washed. Then we had to pick the leaves, wash and prepare them. It was a lot of work.'

Antonio fondly recalls his early start in cheesemaking. 'One day, when I was just ten years old, my father was not home, and a customer came to our family cheese shop asking for burrata. I panicked, but did not want to disappoint him, so I decided to try it. I rolled up my sleeves, relied on my intuition and the skills I had observed from my family, and crafted my first burrata. It turned out to be a massive 4.5 kg cheese, made by accident but marking my debut in the family tradition.'

RIGHT Antonio Asselta at his house in Margherita di Savoia, Puglia

From 1928, Francesco Asselta started making burrata in his family home, in the heart of Andria.

From 1935 to 1975, Francesco and his brother Cosimo produced burrata in their family's two factories. For decades, they remained the sole producers of this unique cheese, sharing its creamy delight with the world.

The family's burrata was enjoyed far and wide, reaching cities like Bologna, Rome, Milan and Oceania. 'We sold several burrata a week, each one kilo or bigger. We sent twenty big burrata a week to the Shah of Persia,' Antonio recalls with pride. At double the price of plain mozzarella, burrata was a luxury item that only the wealthy could afford. 'There was no refrigeration, so only important people could get it,' Antonio explains.

'Despite modern advancements, burrata remains a luxury item today because of the labour. Burrata is still considered one of the best ten cheeses worldwide. The top three positions are held by Italian cheeses: first is Parmigiano, second is gorgonzola, and third is burrata,' Antonio proudly states.

Antonio's story is steeped in familial pride, highlighting the dedication and craftsmanship that have made burrata a symbol of Italian culinary artistry. His reflections show a deep appreciation for the artisanal techniques that have stood the test of time and the innovations that will carry these traditions forward. 'The future of artisanal cheese lies in our ability to tell a story through our products. Every piece of cheese we make carries the legacy of our ancestors and the promise of future generations who will continue this beautiful craft,' Antonio concludes.

ABOVE Asselta Family cheese shop in Andria, Puglia

Giorgio Linguanti agrees. 'As the world becomes more industrialised, the challenge for artisanal cheesemakers is to maintain the quality and authenticity of our products. It's about balancing tradition with innovation, preserving the old methods while embracing innovative technologies to enhance our craft.'

Whether you support the story of Antonio's playful invention or Lorenzo's wintery innovation, one thing remains clear – burrata is a true testament to the rich dairy heritage of Andria. This rich, creamy cheese symbolises the passion of the cheesemakers who crafted it. Each bite carries with it the legacy of these artisans, their stories interwoven into the very fabric of this beloved delicacy.

Burrata's journey from a regional specialty in Puglia to a beloved global delicacy is a narrative of gastronomic exploration and appreciation. As travel and trade barriers reduced in the late twentieth and early twenty-first centuries, so did the confines around regional cuisines. Chefs worldwide began seeking unique, high-quality ingredients that could elevate their creations, leading them to discover the rich dairy traditions of Italy.

Giorgio Linguanti reflects, 'The global spread of burrata can be attributed to its unique texture and flavour profile, which captured the imaginations of chefs and gourmets alike. Its soft, creamy interior, contrasting with the firm outer shell, offers a food experience that transcends cultural and geographical boundaries. Burrata symbolised luxury and artisanal excellence. This cheese has a way of connecting people through its simple yet extraordinary nature.'

The rise of food media and gourmet tourism further boosted burrata's international acclaim. Food enthusiasts travelled to Italy to pursue authentic experiences, returning home with tales of this exquisite cheese. Simultaneously, cooking shows, food blogs and social media platforms celebrated burrata's versatility and appeal, further cementing its status as a must-have ingredient in contemporary cuisine.

Today, burrata graces the tables of high-end restaurants and homes worldwide, captivating palates and embodying the essence of Italian cheesemaking. Its story is a testament to the power of tradition, innovation and the universal love for food that connects us all.

Giorgio adds, 'Burrata's journey from the farms of Puglia to tables worldwide is a story of passion and perseverance. I truly love this cheesy delicacy and how it offers a rich flavour that spans continents and cuisines. It's a tribute to the artisans who preserve Puglian dairy traditions, crafting a cheese that connects us to Italy's culinary heritage.'

LEFT Antonio Asselta and his cousin at the front of their family's house in Andria

30 TO KNOT, OR NOT TO KNOT

THE ART OF SEALING BURRATA

The art of sealing burrata is a technique passed down through generations of skilled cheesemakers, and there are several different methods used.

One of the most charming and traditional methods of sealing burrata involves hand-tying the cheese with natural materials such as raffia or long blades of grass creating the famous 'knot'. This method not only ensures a secure seal, but also adds an authentic, rustic touch that harks back to simpler times. As the raffia tightens, the pouch takes on its characteristic shape.

For those who prefer a more straightforward approach, food-safe string or twine is an effective alternative. Much like raffia, this method secures the pouch tightly, ensuring the interior remains intact.

In the traditional heartlands of Puglia, and in particular in the town of Andria, the common practice was also to use green asphodel leaves to encase the burrata, adding a unique touch that became a symbol of tradition. This practice also assured freshness – if the asphodel leaf faded in colour, that was an indication that the cheese was no longer fresh.

In contemporary cheese production, the use of real leaves has been discontinued, but some artisans use decorative leaves instead, to mimic the traditional look. The bright green leaves wrapped around the snowy white mozzarella offer a visual promise of the freshness inside.

Another technique is knotting the mozzarella itself by hand. After filling the pouch, the top is twisted and knotted. This method requires skill and precision as the cheesemaker manipulates the soft mozzarella to create a tight seal, resulting in a beautiful self-contained package of creamy goodness.

Artisanal cheesemakers often develop custom mozzarella pouches that can be sealed by twisting or folding without any additional materials, or closed by just pinching to seal.

These techniques showcase the cheesemaker's craftsmanship, creating a burrata that is both functional and aesthetically pleasing.

On a larger scale, heat-sealing machines have revolutionised burrata production. These devices provide a consistent and more hygienic seal without compromising the cheese's quality. This is ideal for mass production, resulting in rows of burrata, each perfectly sealed, ready to bring joy to countless tables.

RIGHT Burrata wrapping at Caseificio Maldera, Bari

Each method of sealing burrata, from the rustic to the modern, reflects the cheesemaker's dedication to preserving the cheese's creamy, delightful heart.

Le Delizie del Latte
CASEIFICIO
Produzione propria
Fucci
Vincenzo
Le Delizie del Latte

TRANSITIONING TO TRADITION

THE CHEESEMAKERS OF ANDRIA

Each cheesemaker has a unique approach to making burrata, highlighting their individual technique and the rich history and evolution of this beloved cheese. The passion that these cheesemakers possess reflects an unwavering commitment to tradition.

From the rustic techniques handed down through generations to the modern adaptations that cater to contemporary palates, the cheesemakers of Andria exemplify the perfect blend of passion and heritage.

LE DELIZIE DEL LATTE

Le Delizie del Latte is a family business nestled in the heart of Andria that prides itself on using traditional methods to create delicious burrata. The owner and head cheesemaker, Vincenzo, began his cheesemaking journey in 2006, formally establishing the business in 2008.

Le Delizie del Latte makes a different style of mozzarella, called Mozzarella anni '60, using the traditional method of adding whey instead of citric acid. This results in a more flavourful mozzarella with less salt and richer in probiotics.

The burrata are completely handmade from start to finish. Vincenzo uses only fresh, locally sourced milk, distinguishing his products from industrial ones that often use milk from various regions, including Germany and Hungary. He also makes his own cream daily to maintain the authenticity and freshness that set his products apart. His commitment to using ancient recipes and local ingredients has earned him a unique position in the market.

Vincenzo focuses on maintaining the quality and authenticity of his products. His burrata is made in small batches and sold by the end of the day, primarily through their deli and some restaurants within Italy.

In a market often dominated by industrial producers, his passion for cheesemaking and dedication to quality make his products stand out.

LEFT Le Delizie del Latte and his owner Vincenzo, Andria

CASEIFICIO EUROPA

This mid-size cheese producer is owned by two brothers, Angelo and Nicola Aruanno, and fuelled by the passion and dedication of the Aruanno family, who have been the cornerstone of the business since its inception.

Caseificio Europa, synonymous with quality and good taste, was founded by Mr Aruanno Emanuele in 1981. After years of working in various dairies around Andria, Emanuele decided to start his own family business. His experience and expertise laid a strong foundation for the business, which would later be continued by his sons, Angelo and Nicola.

Angelo and Nicola, having learned the craft from their father, took over the business in 1997. They have continued the family tradition, passing on the craftsmanship to their kids who work within the business with the same level of professionalism and dedication, while evolving from using a completely manual process to a semi-automated one, maintaining the high standards and quality. The brothers emphasise the importance of understanding milk to create high-quality cheese, a philosophy encapsulated by Angelo:

> **'Being a cheesemaker** means knowing how to understand milk in order to produce everything possible, starting from white gold.'

Their burrata are closed by hand, but the outer mozzarella shell is produced by machine, and they also have a machine to fill the burrata with stracciatella, bringing greater consistency and efficiency to the process.

Caseificio Europa use raffia to tie their burrata, a nod to traditional methods that enhance the authenticity and appeal of their products. The family have their own farm and milk supply, ensuring control over the quality of their ingredients from start to finish.

The Aruanno brothers sell their burrata to restaurants all over Italy and France, where their commitment to quality and tradition is recognised and appreciated. Their journey from having a small store in Andria to becoming a trusted name in the European food scene is a testament to their hard work, passion and dedication to the art of cheesemaking.

LEFT Caseificio Europa and Nicola Aruanno, Andria

RIGHT Caseificio Maldera, Bari

CASEIFICIO MALDERA

Caseificio Maldera in Corato highlights a remarkable blend of tradition and innovation. Founded in 1972 by Giuseppe Maldera, this family-run business has grown into a top-level brand, recognised for its authentic Puglian dairy products.

The milk is processed just hours after milking, providing a unique taste. Seventy-five per cent of their milk comes from controlled breeding in Puglia and Basilicata, ensuring high-quality, genuine dairy products.

Caseificio Maldera produces an impressive 200,000 burrata per day. Most are produced by fully automated machines, but they also make burrata by hand, hand-tied with string, and even have a premium burrata, which is encased in the traditional leaf and hand-tied to form its characteristic tuft.

Their point of difference is really the versatility in being able to produce so many different types of burrata to cater for all market needs. Caseificio Maldera distribute to supermarkets and restaurants all over Europe.

While their journey began with classic burrata, over time, they have evolved to introduce flavoured variations, such as truffle, blue-vein and smoked, catering to more modern tastes while maintaining authenticity. This evolution demonstrates their commitment to innovation and exploration.

AZIENDA AGRICOLA QUERCETA

Nestled in the countryside of Putignano, one hour from Andria, Querceta is a fully certified organic farm that is home to the entire production process, starting from the field where the dairy cows graze, through milking and then to the production of dairy products. They also produce their own meat, olive oil and vegetables.

At Querceta, the milk doesn't get pasteurised or homogenised, and the cheeses are processed by hand following the experience and traditions of the Puglian master cheesemakers. Their organic burrata is just one of their many products, with some of their cheese aged up to 24 months in the cellar.

ABOVE AND RIGHT
Cheese aging room and mozzarella making at Azienda Agricola Querceta, Putignano

This organic farm proves that the art of cheesemaking begins not in the dairy, but in the pasture, where the milk quality sets the foundation for the cheese's flavour, texture and nutritional value.

IN THE PASTURES

42 IMPORTANCE OF MILK

Milk, the primary raw material in cheesemaking, reflects the land's health, the livestock's diet and the farming traditions. It carries within it the unique environmental conditions, including soil, climate and topography, that give agricultural products distinctive characteristics.

The importance of milk in cheesemaking cannot be overstated. Every aspect of milk, from its fat content and protein structure to the presence of natural enzymes and bacteria, plays a crucial role in determining the final outcome. The fat globules in milk contribute to the creaminess and flavour, while the proteins casein and whey determine the cheese's structure and texture. Furthermore, the natural sugars in milk are essential for fermentation, which is pivotal in developing the cheese's flavour profile.

> **'The terroir of the land, the diet of our cows, and the care we put into milking, these elements are all captured in the milk,** which is the soul of our cheese. Without this foundation, we wouldn't have the same depth of flavour and texture. That's what makes burrata so special,' shared Irene from Querceta.

From a nutritional and flavour point of view, milk from animals grazing on diverse herbs is more complex than milk from animals fed in barns.

The grass plays a crucial role in the milk quality, and most farmers spend a lot of time managing the grass and the animals' diet, as it is a fundamental element in determining milk and cheese quality.

As the season changes, the grass changes and more mature plants contribute to heavier molecules that give the milk, and therefore the cheese, a more persistent flavour.

'The balance of fat, protein and natural sugars in the milk is crucial. It's what gives burrata its signature creaminess and structure. You must work with the milk, not against it, allowing its natural properties to guide the cheesemaking process,' Giorgio explains.

This deep appreciation for the raw materials and meticulous processes involved highlights the artistry of cheesemaking. It's a craft rooted in the land and in the lives of the animals that produce the milk.

COW BREEDS & CHARACTERISTICS

The composition of milk is greatly altered depending on the type of breed, wellbeing, stage of lactation and age as well as environmental factors such as hygiene, climate, feed and season.

PODOLICA

Podolica cows are a rare breed native to Italy, known for their ability to thrive in harsh environments and utilise otherwise unusable food resources, such as shrub-covered grazing areas. Their milk is not produced in large quantities, but it is highly valued for its richness and quality. It is particularly suitable for making traditional Italian cheeses, including caciocavallo and burrata.

The milk from Podolica cows has a high fat content, which contributes to the texture of burrata. The robust and natural diet of these cows, combined with their unique genetic traits, ensures that the milk is not only flavourful but also rich in nutrients, enhancing the overall quality of the cheese.

BRUNA ITALIANA (ALPINA)

Known for its high-quality milk, the Bruna Italiana breed produces milk with an excellent balance of fat and protein, making it suitable for both hard and soft cheese production. This versatile milk is appreciated for its consistency and richness, which contribute to the flavour and texture of cheeses like Asiago, fontina and taleggio. The Bruna Italiana is a cornerstone in Italian dairy farming, supporting a diverse range of cheese types.

HOLSTEIN-FRIESIAN

Predominantly found in the US, Europe, Australia and New Zealand, the Holstein-Friesian breed stands as a pillar of the global dairy industry due to its exceptional milk production. Originating from the Netherlands and northern Germany, this breed has been optimised for high-volume milk yield. Celebrated in Australia for its significant contribution to the dairy sector, Holstein-Friesians produce milk with lower fat content, ideal for softer cheeses and with protein levels that provide a clean, mild flavour profile. These large cattle typically have black and white or red and white colour patterns and a robust stature. Holstein-Friesians are valued for their adaptability and efficiency on Australian dairy farms, pivotal in meeting the increasing demand for domestic and international dairy products.

RIGHT Podolica and Friesian cows in Puglia, Italy

JERSEY

Originating from the Isle of Jersey (off the northwest coast of France), Jersey cattle are arguably one of the most attractive cow breeds, with large eyes, a pale caramel coat, black nose and black markings on their muzzle, ears and feet. Their popularity, however, is not just due to their appearance. Jersey milk boasts the highest fat content (approx. 6%) of any breed, and higher protein levels (approx 3.5%) than other dairy breeds. This means more cream per litre of Jersey milk, ultimately translating to more cheese!

Jersey milk is known for its creaminess and superior flavour, and is ideal for making various cheeses, including hard cheeses like cheddar and gouda, and soft cheeses like camembert, brie, blue cheese, mozzarella and butterkäse. Jerseys contribute significantly to the local dairy industry, providing an essential ingredient and helping meet the growing demand for high-quality dairy.

In the art of cheesemaking, the choice of cow breed is crucial. Each breed brings distinct qualities to the milk, shaping the character of the cheese. The variations in fat and protein content play a vital role in determining the cheese's flavour, texture, yield and nutritional profile.

AUSTRALIAN RED

Integral to Australia's dairy industry, the Australian Red, also known as the 'Aussie Red', is praised for its resilience, adaptability and premium milk quality. Originating from Scandinavian breeds, these medium-sized cows, which are primarily red with white markings, have evolved to thrive in Australia's diverse climates.

They produce high-yield, protein-rich and butterfat-laden milk, ideal for cheesemaking. Aussie Reds are noted for their robust health and efficiency, making their milk especially valued by artisanal cheesemakers, who use it to create luxurious cheeses like burrata. As the demand for high-quality local cheese grows, the Aussie Red stands at the forefront of Australia's dairy excellence, promising a sustainable and prosperous future for the industry.

LEFT Jersey cows in Gippsland, Australia

48 ULTRA-HIGH TEMPERATURE VS FRESH CREAM

The choice between ultra-high temperature (UHT) cream and fresh cream in burrata making is significant, affecting the flavour, texture and overall quality of the cheese. Each type of cream has its own characteristics, and understanding these differences is crucial for any dedicated cheesemaker.

Fresh cream is often celebrated for its pure, rich flavour. It retains all the natural enzymes and bacteria that contribute to fermentation, allowing for a more complex and nuanced flavour profile. Its natural sweetness and high-fat content are perfect for cheeses like burrata, where creaminess and depth of flavour are paramount.

> **'Working with fresh cream feels like working with a living ingredient** – it evolves and changes, adding layers of authenticity and character to the cheese,' explains Giorgio.

In contrast, UHT cream is sterilised at ultra-high temperatures. This high-heat treatment removes natural enzymes and bacteria, resulting in a cream with a longer shelf life but a more subdued flavour. While UHT cream lacks the depth and complexity of fresh cream, it can be effectively used in cheesemaking, especially in industrial settings where consistency and storage stability are vital considerations.

The choice between UHT and fresh cream depends on the cheesemaker's priorities and production needs. For those dedicated to preserving the rich artisanal traditions of cheesemaking, fresh cream remains the preferred choice. It captures the essence of the terroir and the meticulous care involved in each step of the process, from pasture to plate.

However, UHT cream has its place in modern cheesemaking. Its stability and ease of use make it a practical option for large-scale producers, and for applications where the variability of fresh cream could pose challenges.

'In my practice, I deeply appreciate fresh cream's complexities. It is a testament to the land, the livestock and the time-honoured techniques that define true artisanal cheese. Yet I also recognise the value of UHT cream in ensuring that high-quality cheese can reach a broader audience without compromising safety and consistency,' Giorgio declares.

Ultimately, the art of cheesemaking is about balancing tradition with innovation. Whether using fresh cream for its rich, evolving flavours, or UHT cream for its practicality and stability, the goal remains: to create a cheese that honours the past while embracing the future.

RIGHT Stracciatella Making, Andria

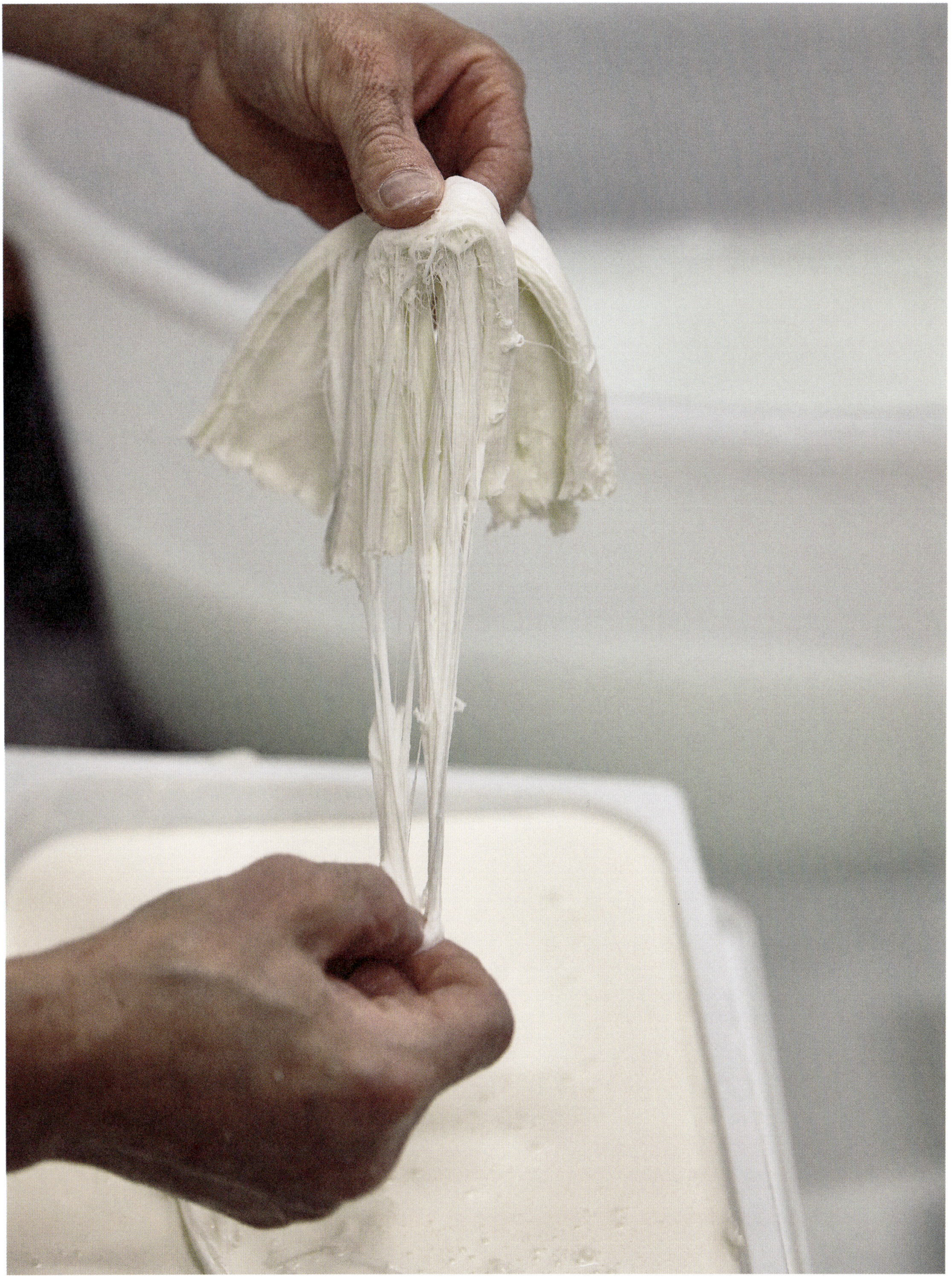

Le Delizie del Latte
CASEIFICIO

FORMAGGIO VACCHINO CROTONESE
€ 8,90 AL KG
OLANDESE EURO 7.90 AL KG.
10,90
GRANA PADANO
STAGIONATURA 12 MESI
PECORINO DI CORATO
FORMAGGIO TENERELLO DI CAPRA EURO 14.90 AL KG.
FORMAGGIO CASERECCIO EURO 11.90 AL KG.
FORMAGGIO DI CORATO EURO 12.90 AL KG.
PROVOLETTE AURICCHIO EURO 13.80 AL KG.

CHEESE IN CULTURE

A BLEND OF TRADITION & INNOVATION

With its creamy heart and delicate mozzarella shell, burrata holds a special place in Italian cuisine. While its origins lie in the sun-drenched fields of Puglia, this exquisite cheese has made its way across various regions of Italy, each adding its unique touch to how burrata is enjoyed.

The traditional way to savour burrata is simple – with a drizzle of high-quality extra-virgin olive oil, a sprinkle of sea salt and a slice of crusty bread. This minimalist approach allows the cheese's natural flavours to shine. In Puglia, it's often enjoyed with fresh tomatoes and basil, reminiscent of the classic Caprese salad. The sweetness of ripe tomatoes, the aromatic punch of basil and the creaminess of burrata create a harmonious blend that epitomises the simplicity of Italian cuisine.

In contrast, in northern Italy, burrata takes on a richer pairing. Here, it's served with earthy roasted vegetables such as beets and artichokes, or alongside hearty grains like farro and barley, adding a creamy, luxurious touch. These combinations reflect the region's love of robust flavours and textures.

Giorgio shares his favourite way to enjoy burrata:
'I love pairing burrata with seasonal fruits like figs and peaches. The sweetness of the fruit complements the rich creaminess of the cheese, creating a perfect balance. Drizzle a bit of honey and some crushed nuts like pistachios or hazelnuts, and you have a dish that's simple yet incredibly indulgent.'

The versatility of burrata extends beyond traditional Italian pairings. In contemporary cuisine, chefs around the world have embraced this cheese's unique qualities, incorporating it into innovative dishes that span diverse culinary traditions.

Travel north to Campania, and burrata will be incorporated into more complex dishes. Here, chefs might use it to top a margherita pizza, where the cheese's creaminess balances the tangy tomato sauce and the aromatic basil.

In Rome, burrata finds its place in modern Italian cuisine. Chefs use it to elevate classic pasta dishes, such as spaghetti alla carbonara or rigatoni all'Amatriciana, where the cheese's creamy core melds with rich Roman sauces, creating a decadent dining experience.

LEFT Fresh tomatoes from a local market in Rome

‘Burrata’s versatility makes it so special. Whether in a traditional or contemporary dish, it always adds an element of surprise and delight,’ says Giorgio.

The Veneto region, known for its gastronomical innovation, has embraced burrata in unexpected ways. Here, it might be served with seafood, such as mussels, shrimp or scallops, its creaminess complementing the delicate sweetness of the shellfish. The combination of burrata and fresh seafood is a revelation. It showcases the cheese’s ability to adapt and enhance different flavours, making it a star in any dish.

Burrata’s popularity has spread far beyond Italy’s borders, captivating chefs and food enthusiasts worldwide. In Australia, burrata has found a home on the menus of top restaurants and in the hearts of food lovers. This creamy delicacy has journeyed from the pastoral farms of Puglia to the finest dining tables around the globe, inspiring chefs and delighting diners. It embodies the rich traditions of Italian dairy farming while embracing new and innovative culinary practices. Whether enjoyed in its homeland or in a distant corner of the world, burrata remains a symbol of the enduring appeal of artisanal craftsmanship and the joy of sharing good food.

RIGHT Monopoli, Puglia

CHIARA

60 FILLED BURRATA

A MODERN TWIST ON A CLASSIC DELIGHT

Filled burrata represents a delicious innovation in the world of traditional Italian cheese, bringing an added layer of complexity and flavour to this beloved dairy product. Both Caseificio Maldera and Massari Mozzarella Bar in Puglia have embraced this modern twist, enhancing burrata's rich, creamy interior with a variety of gourmet fillings.

At Caseificio Maldera, filled burratas include truffle burrata, which infuses the cheese with an earthy, aromatic depth, and blue-veined burrata, offering a tangy, robust contrast to the traditional creaminess. This creative approach showcases the cheesemaker's willingness to innovate and cater to contemporary palates.

Similarly, Massari Mozzarella Bar takes pride in its filled burrata offerings, pushing the boundaries of flavour combinations. Their filled burrata can feature ingredients such as sun-dried tomatoes, pesto, tuna or spicy salami, creating a unique blend of tastes that burst with every bite. These filled burratas are perfect for gourmet salads or antipasto platters, or simply enjoyed on their own, bringing a touch of luxury to any meal.

Giorgio Linguanti reflects, 'Filled burrata is a wonderful evolution of the traditional recipe, offering an exquisite surprise with each bite. By incorporating ingredients like truffles, chocolate or sun-dried tomatoes, we not only preserve the heritage of Italian cheesemaking but also bring new and exciting flavours to the table.'

The range of burrata flavours available today is truly impressive. Beyond the classic versions, you can now find smoked burrata (affumicata), caprese burrata with tomato and basil, pistachio mortadella burrata, truffle burrata, prosciutto stracciatella burrata, and even sweet variations like Nutella burrata. Other creative options include pesto, tuna, maple syrup and prosciutto crudo. Each variation adds a unique twist to the traditional burrata, making it a versatile and luxurious choice for any culinary creation.

RIGHT Filled burrata at Massarí Mozzarella Bar, Polignano a Mare

THE ARTISAN'S TOUCH

64 TRADITION MEETS TECHNOLOGY

HANDCRAFTED VS. MACHINE-MADE BURRATA

Burrata, with its luxurious texture and rich flavour, is a cheese that holds a special place in the hearts of many. In production, however, there are two distinct paths: the traditional handcrafting method and the modern machine-made approach. Each method offers its own unique qualities, reflecting a blend of time-honoured techniques and contemporary innovations.

MAKING BURRATA BY HAND

Crafting burrata by hand is an art form that embodies the tradition of Italian cheesemaking. The process begins with the preparation of fresh mozzarella curds, which are stretched and kneaded until they achieve the desired consistency. This curd is then divided, with some portions set aside to create the stracciatella. The remaining curd is carefully formed into small pouches that will serve as the outer shell of the burrata.

The creation of the stracciatella involves meticulously tearing the mozzarella curds into fine shreds and mixing them with fresh cream. This filling is then delicately placed into each mozzarella pouch. Once the pouches are filled, they are sealed with a twist or a knot tie, or with the heat of hot water, encasing the stracciatella within. Each step requires a practised hand and an eye for detail, as the texture and quality of the final product depend heavily on the skill of the cheesemaker. The result is a burrata that is unique, with slight variations that reflect the artisanal touch of its creator.

RIGHT Burrata filling at Le Delizie del Latte, Andria

MAKING BURRATA BY MACHINE

Making burrata by machine involves a more standardised and efficient process, designed to meet higher production demands while maintaining quality. The initial steps are similar, with fresh mozzarella curds being stretched and kneaded. However, automation takes over much of the labour-intensive work. Machines precisely measure and mix the curds and cream to create the stracciatella, ensuring consistency in every batch.

Forming and filling the mozzarella pouches is also mechanised. Advanced machinery can shape and seal the burrata quickly and uniformly, producing large quantities in a fraction of the time required to do so by hand. While this method sacrifices some of the artisanal nuances of handcrafting, it results in high-quality burrata that is accessible to a broader market. The consistency and efficiency of machine-made burrata ensures it can be enjoyed far beyond its traditional Puglian origins.

BALANCING TRADITION AND INNOVATION

Both methods of making burrata – by hand and by machine – play crucial roles in preserving and promoting this beloved cheese. Handcrafted burrata celebrates the cheese's rich heritage, while machine-made burrata ensures it can be enjoyed by a wider audience, maintaining quality and consistency and meeting the demands of modern production.

Each method brings its own strengths to the table, ensuring that this delicious cheese remains a cherished part of gourmet traditions around the world.

MAROTTA EVOLUTION

Located in Northern Italy, in the town of Nonantola near Modena, the Marotta Evolution Group are the world's sole manufacturer and marketer of machines for the automatic production of burrata.

The Marotta brothers, Carmine and Fabio, who have more than seventeen years of experience in industrial automation, have established and implemented the detailed technology and equipment that fully automates the burrata manufacturing process.

Being such a delicate cheese to craft, these complex machines allow the pulled curd to be shaped into a pouch, which is then automatically filled with stringy bits of mozzarella and fresh cream before being secured by a specialised knot.

This method of automation not only ensures that the company can cater to growing demand in Italy, Europe and internationally, it also ensures that companies can adhere to strict health and safety measures on a global scale.

LEFT Burrata machine, That's Amore Cheese

STEP-BY-STEP GUIDE TO MAKING BURRATA

Not only is burrata the most delicious cheese, it is surprisingly easy to make.

In this step-by-step guide you will learn how to prepare the mozzarella curds, shape and stretch the mozzarella pouch, make the luscious stracciatella filling and, finally, to shape and seal the perfect burrata.

INGREDIENTS

5 L (169 fl oz) full-fat unhomogenised milk, cold
7.5 g (¼ oz) citric acid (1.5 g/$\frac{1}{32}$ oz per litre), dissolved in 60 ml (2 fl oz) of cool water
1 ml rennet (mixed with a little water to aid distribution through the milk)
150 g (5½ oz) fresh thick (double/heavy) cream

MAKING THE CURD

To make the curd, pour the milk into a saucepan. Warm over a low heat on the stove and add the citric acid while stirring.

Heat the milk to 37°C (100°F), constantly stirring, then remove from the heat and stir the rennet through.

Cover the pot and leave to set for 25–30 minutes, until the mixture reaches a gel-like consistency.

Test consistency and cut the curd into 2 cm (¾ in) cubes, stir gently and transfer to a colander to drain for approximately 5–10 minutes.

STRETCHING THE CURD

To stretch the curds, fill a bowl with cold water and keep it nearby.

Transfer half of the drained curd into a bowl and gently break it apart with your fingers, then add 130 g (4½ oz) salt.

Over a low heat, warm approximately 2 L (68 fl oz) water until it reaches 85–90°C (185–195°F). Pour the water into the bowl until the curds are submerged.

Using two flat wooden spoons, gently stir and press the curds together until they join into a solid mass.

Still using the spoons, stretch the curd until it is smooth and pliable. You want it to look glossy.

CONTINUED OVERLEAF

Pour milk

Add citric acid & heat

Add rennet

Test and cut curds

Stir curds

Drain

Add salt

Add boiling water

Stretch

Shape into a rope and place in water

Tear into shreds

Add cream and season

Repeat stretching process

Form a disc and fill

Close by twisting

MAKING STRACCIATELLA

Shape the mozzarella into a rope and place in cold water for a few minutes. Tear it into thin strands like string cheese. Add the cream, and season with a pinch of salt. Mix together and set aside, this will be your stracciatella filling.

MAKING BURRATA

Now make the mozzarella case for the burrata. Transfer the remaining curds into a bowl and repeat the stretching process until you get a glossy mozzarella.

To shape the burrata, take a chunk of curd and stretch it. Flatten it into a disc about 15 cm (6 in) wide and 0.5 cm (¼ in) thick.

Holding the disc in your hand, spoon the stracciatella mixture into the centre, pushing down gently.

Pull the edges of the disc over the top and close the burrata by twisting it into a knot, dipping the top into the boiling water to help seal it.

Place the completed burrata in cold water and repeat the process until all the curd has been used.

WAYS TO CLOSE THE BURRATA

WITH A KNOT This method involves closing the burrata with a simple knot on top.

WITHOUT A KNOT This simpler method involves closing the burrata by pinching the top and removing the excess curd, making it look like a mozzarella ball.

ANDRIA-STYLE Named after the town of its origin, this traditional shape is tied with string.

STORING BURRATA CORRECTLY

If you have made your own burrata, storing it correctly is imperative. Burrata will last up to five days in the fridge, but the sooner you eat it, the better. To maintain freshness and prevent it from drying out, it's best to store burrata in its original liquid in a sealed container. It's best to consume it all once you have cut into it; however, if you need to store it once cut, gently wrap the cut burrata in plastic wrap, making sure that it is completely covered and that there are no holes or gaps.

Avoid storing burrata in the freezer. Freezing noticeably worsens the texture and taste of burrata.

THE RECIPE COLLECTION

RECIPE CREATORS

CHEF CARLOS NASPIRAN

Carlos Naspiran, head chef at That's Amore Cheese in Melbourne, Victoria, has enriched this book with his beautiful range of recipes that showcase burrata in various innovative ways.

At the age of three, Carlos discovered his passion for food in the rustic kitchen of his grandmother's countryside home in Bogota, Colombia. The joy of smelling and eating freshly baked bread and picking vegetables from the garden with his grandmother nurtured a deep-seated passion for cooking that would shape his future.

Today, as a master of his craft, Carlos finds endless inspiration in burrata. 'Burrata's versatility inspires me to innovate and create dishes that highlight its creamy texture in new and exciting ways. I love challenging the misconception that burrata is only for cold dishes by showcasing its potential in warm dishes. It's a beautiful way to blend tradition with contemporary cooking techniques,' says Carlos.

Working with burrata has encouraged Carlos to experiment and get creative. At That's Amore Cheese, his work with burrata and other cheeses is a tribute to tradition, blending his past with his present culinary explorations.

Carlos's ability to honour his heritage while pushing the boundaries of how burrata can be used reflects his passion and dedication to cheesemaking. Through his recipes, Carlos invites us to experience burrata in new and exciting ways, celebrating the rich flavours and textures of this exquisite cheese.

CHEF SALIM GAFAYRI

Salim Gafayri's journey began in his hometown of Izmir, Turkey. At the age of fifteen he moved to Australia, embarking on a life-changing adventure. This move sparked his passion for pizza-making, ignited by his first job at an Italian pizzeria.

By 2020, Salim was fully immersed in the art of pizza-making, becoming a recognised face at Arbory Afloat. His expertise spans a diverse range of pizza styles, including Neapolitan, New York, Detroit and focaccia. Salim's dedication to his craft and exceptional pizzas have delighted countless patrons.

In this book, Salim Gafayri has contributed as a guest pizza chef, sharing his pizza dough recipe and his unique flavour combination, highlighting the luxurious texture of burrata with his masterful pizza-making techniques. These are sure to delight and inspire home cooks and professionals alike.

Salim's career is a testament to his passion, skill and dedication. His story, recipes and love for the art of pizza-making bring a unique and flavourful dimension to this book, celebrating the fusion of traditional Italian cheese with innovative pizza creations.

RIGHT Chef Carlos Naspiran, Melbourne

UGO BURRATA BAR

Ugo Burrata Bar at the South Melbourne Market is a destination for burrata lovers. Opened in December 2023, this concept takes the simple, yet beautiful That's Amore Cheese burrata and pairs it with changing seasonal ingredients to create delectable dishes that demonstrate the many ways burrata can be enjoyed.

In a bagel, on toast, as part of a salad and even for dessert, burrata is served on everything here. A selection of Burrata Bar recipes are featured in this book for you to enjoy and experiment with at home.

'We want to showcase that burrata and mozzarella are not only seasonal products, but delicious ingredients that can be paired up all year round,' says co-owner and co-founder Dario Di Clerico.

CHEF DARIO DI CLERICO

Dario Di Clerico, Giorgio Linguanti's close friend and collaborator, has brought a wealth of culinary expertise to the table, enriching the burrata experience with his innovative and fun recipes, and opening the first burrata bar in Australia in 2023, in partnership with Giorgio.

Growing up in Italy before later moving to Melbourne, Dario has embraced fresh, seasonal Victorian ingredients and begun exploring new horizons. His 'paddock to plate' philosophy drove him to create traditional Abruzzese dishes with a modern twist.

Teaming up with Giorgio Linguanti at That's Amore Cheese, Dario's creativity and flavour expertise paired perfectly with Giorgio's artisanal cheeses.

Dario loves to experiment and get creative with burrata, drawing on his previous experience working at Michelin-star restaurants and his passion for using local produce.

Dario's innovative burrata recipes throughout this book reflect his dedication to quality and creativity. His recipes showcase burrata's potential in both traditional and contemporary dishes while adding a little bit of flair.

Welcome to the heart of our culinary journey, where the magic of burrata unfolds across every meal. From delightful breakfasts that start your day with a creamy burst of flavour to indulgent sweets that provide the perfect ending, each recipe celebrates the versatility and richness of this beloved cheese. Whether you're looking to elevate your starters, enhance your mains or add a special touch to your pasta and sides, these recipes will inspire and delight.

Buon appetito!

1

BREAKFAST

SERVES 1

BURRATA BAGEL

INGREDIENTS

BAGEL

250 ml (8½ fl oz) warm water
1 tablespoon sugar
7 g (¼ oz) active dry yeast
300 g (10½ oz) bread flour or plain (all-purpose) flour
1 teaspoon salt

BAGEL TOPPINGS

poppy seeds
sesame seeds
sea salt flakes

TO SERVE

2 rashers (slices) bacon
2 eggs
1 mini (60 g/2 oz) burrata
extra-virgin olive oil, to drizzle

METHOD

To make the bagels, in a bowl, mix the warm water and sugar, then sprinkle the yeast over the top. Let it sit for 5–10 minutes until foamy.

In a separate large mixing bowl, combine the bread flour and salt, giving it a quick stir to combine. Pour in the yeast mixture and mix well until a dough forms.

Transfer the dough to a lightly floured surface and knead well for about 10 minutes, until the dough is smooth and elastic. Transfer to a lightly oiled bowl, cover with plastic wrap and allow to rise for about 1 hour, or until it has doubled in size.

Remove the dough from the bowl and divide it into 8 equal pieces. Use your hands to roll each piece of dough into a ball, then use your finger to poke a hole through the centre. Carefully stretch out the hole a little to make the ball into a bagel shape. Repeat until all the dough has been shaped.

Preheat the oven to 220°C (430°F). Bring a large pot of water to the boil. Carefully boil each bagel for 1–2 minutes on each side, then remove with a slotted spoon and place on a lined baking tray.

Add your toppings, then bake for 15–20 minutes, or until the bagels have turned golden brown.

Allow to cool for a few minutes before serving.

In a frying pan, cook the bacon for about 5–6 minutes, until crisp, then set aside to drain on paper towel. In the same pan, fry the eggs for about 2 minutes, until the whites are fully cooked but the yolks are soft and creamy, then season with salt and black pepper. In the meantime, halve a bagel and toast it.

TO ASSEMBLE Lay the bagel halves on a plate and butter them if desired, then add the bacon. Top the bacon with the eggs and then the burrata. Drizzle with olive oil and season with salt and pepper.

SERVES 6

86 BURRATA FRITTATA

INGREDIENTS

2 potatoes, dice into 1 cm (½ in)
12 eggs
120 ml (4 fl oz) pouring (single/light) cream
50 g (1¾ oz) parmesan cheese, grated
2 red capsicums (bell peppers), julienned
1 medium onion, julienned
olive oil, for frying and drizzling
180 g (6½ oz) smoked scamorza, cut into 1 cm (½ in) dice
1 × 125 g (4½ oz) burrata
black pepper

METHOD

Boil the potatoes in water with salt until they are cooked through, then strain and set aside to dry.

While the potatoes are drying, combine the eggs, cream and parmesan in a bowl. Whisk until the ingredients are well incorporated, then set aside.

Cook the capsicum and onion in a frying pan with a splash of olive oil until tender. Add a pinch of salt and set aside.

Preheat the oven to 180°C (360°F) fan-forced. Add the potatoes, capsicum, onion and smoked scamorza to the egg mixture, making sure everything is well combined.

In a large ovenproof frying pan, heat a drizzle of olive oil, making sure the oil coats the entire surface of the pan. Take the pan off the heat, then add the frittata mix and spread evenly using a spatula. Cook in the oven for 10–15 minutes, or until the frittata is cooked through.

Remove from the oven and let the frittata rest for a couple of minutes. Place the burrata on top, then drizzle with olive oil and season with salt and black pepper. Serve immediately.

SERVES 4

88

BURRATA ON TOAST WITH RHUBARB, CITRUS, SWEET RICOTTA & PISTACHIOS

INGREDIENTS

4 slices bread
4 mini (60 g/2 oz) burratas
12 grapefruit segments
12 orange segments
4 tablespoons crushed pistachios
mint leaves, to garnish

SWEET RICOTTA

500 g (1 lb 2 oz) ricotta
25 g (1 oz) caster (superfine) sugar
½ tablespoon olive oil

POACHED RHUBARB

150 g (5½ oz) caster (superfine) sugar
150 ml (5 fl oz) water
1 star anise
8 strips orange peel
13 sticks of rhubarb, cut into 5 cm (2 in) batons

METHOD

To make the sweet ricotta, mix the ricotta, sugar and olive oil in a blender until smooth.

Next, make the poached rhubarb. Preheat the oven to 180°C (360°F). Place the sugar, water, star anise and orange peel in an ovenproof saucepan and bring the mixture to the boil. Add the rhubarb, then cover the pan with foil and place in the oven for 5 minutes, or until the sticks are cooked (they should keep their structure). Be careful, they can overcook very quickly.

Set aside to cool, reserving the poaching liquid.

TO SERVE Toast the bread, then spread with some of the sweet ricotta. Place a burrata in the middle of each slice, then scatter the grapefruit and orange segments around. Add the poached rhubarb, sprinkle with crushed pistachios, garnish with mint and drizzle some of the rhubarb poaching liquid over the top.

SERVES 3

POACHED EGGS ON TOAST

INGREDIENTS

CAPSICUM RICOTTA

2 large red capsicums (bell peppers), julienned
450 g (1 lb) ricotta
black pepper
1 tablespoon red wine vinegar
1½ tablespoons olive oil

9 asparagus spears
olive oil
3 large heirloom tomatoes, cut into wedges
3 slices ciabatta, toasted
3 eggs, poached
3 mini (60 g/2 oz) burratas
smoked paprika, for dusting
15 g (½ oz) toasted almond flakes
15 basil leaves

METHOD

To make the capsicum ricotta, place the capsicums in a frying pan with a drizzle of olive oil and cook over a medium heat until tender, then set aside to cool. Once cool, combine the capsicums with the ricotta, salt, pepper, red wine vinegar and olive oil in a blender and blend until the mixture forms a creamy and silky puree.

Bring a saucepan of water with a tablespoon of salt to the boil, then add the asparagus. Blanch them for 1 minute, drain, then grill them in a chargrill pan with some olive oil and black pepper. Set aside.

Put the tomatoes in a bowl and season with salt, olive oil and black pepper.

TO SERVE Place the toasted ciabatta on plates, then add a generous amount of the capsicum ricotta to each slice. Place the poached eggs on top of the ricotta, then arrange the grilled asparagus, tomatoes and burratas around each piece of toast. To finish, dust with smoked paprika, then garnish with almond flakes and basil leaves.

SERVES 2

92 RICOTTA PANCAKES WITH MIXED BERRIES

INGREDIENTS

icing (confectioners') sugar, for dusting
2 mini (60 g/2 oz) burratas
80 g (2¾ oz) strawberries, sliced
80 g (2¾ oz) raspberries
80 g (2¾ oz) blueberries
100 g (3½ oz) crushed pistachios

PANCAKE BATTER

100 g (3½ oz) buffalo ricotta
200 ml (7 fl oz) milk
1 egg
1 teaspoon vanilla extract
100 g (3½ oz) plain wholemeal (whole-wheat) flour
1 teaspoon baking powder
1 teaspoon bicarbonate of soda (baking soda)
50 g (1¾ oz) caster (superfine) sugar

BERRY COULIS

200 g (7 oz) frozen mixed berries
70 g (2½ oz) caster (superfine) sugar

METHOD

To make the batter, mix the ricotta, milk, egg and vanilla extract until the ricotta is dissolved, then add the dry ingredients and mix until you have obtained a smooth batter.

To make the berry coulis, mix the berries and sugar in a saucepan and cook, stirring, over a medium–high heat until the sugar has dissolved, then set aside to cool. Once the mixture has cooled, pass it through a sieve, then set aside.

Preheat the oven to 180°C (360°F) fan-forced. Take two 12 cm (4¾ in) non-stick, ovenproof pans and warm them in the oven prior to cooking. Once the pans are warm, add the pancake batter until each pan is almost full but not overflowing. Cook the pancakes in the oven for around 12 minutes or until cooked through – you can check this using a cake tester. Once cooked, turn the pancakes onto a plate and dust with icing sugar.

TO SERVE Spoon some berry coulis into the bottom of each plate, place the pancake on top, then add some more coulis over the top. Place a mini burrata on top of each pancake, then scatter fresh mixed berries around the plate and sprinkle with crushed pistachios.

SERVES 4

SCRAMBLED EGGS WITH AVOCADO & JALAPEÑOS

INGREDIENTS

4 slices bread, toasted
1 jalapeño, thinly sliced
2 avocados, quartered
4 × 90 g (3 oz) burratas
black pepper

SCRAMBLED EGGS

12 eggs
120 ml (4 fl oz) thick (double/heavy) cream
50 g (1¾ oz) Grana Padano, grated
30 g (1 oz) unsalted butter
180 g (6½ oz) corn kernels (fresh or tinned)
1 spring onion (scallion), thinly sliced

PICKLED SHALLOTS

1 shallot (peeled and cut into 4 mm (¼ in) rounds, rings separated)
70 ml (2¼ fl oz) red wine vinegar
70 ml (2¼ fl oz) water
60 g (2 oz) white sugar

HERB OIL

150 ml (5 fl oz) olive oil
½ bunch basil
½ bunch flat-leaf (Italian) parsley
pinch of salt

METHOD

To make the scrambled eggs, mix the eggs, cream, Grana Padano and a pinch of salt in a bowl and whisk until the ingredients are well incorporated.

Melt the butter in a frying pan over a low heat, then sauté the corn and spring onion for 2 minutes, mixing constantly. Add the egg mix and cook, constantly stirring until the mixture is cooked and creamy, but not dry.

Place the shallots in a small heatproof bowl. Combine the vinegar, water and sugar in a small saucepan and bring it to the boil. As soon as the mixture boils, pour it over the shallots and set aside for the shallots to pickle.

For the herb oil, mix all ingredients in a blender until smooth, then transfer to a small saucepan and warm it to 60°C (140°F) – about 1 minute.

Strain the oil through a fine chinois or sieve, then transfer to a bowl. Sit the bowl over another bowl filled with ice and water, to cool the oil rapidly.

TO SERVE Spoon the scrambled eggs over the toast slices, then top with pickled shallots and sliced jalapeño. Place an avocado quarter and a burrata on each plate and season with salt and black pepper. To finish, drizzle some of the herb oil around the plate.

SERVES 4

96 WAFFLES WITH SWEET RICOTTA & BERRIES

INGREDIENTS

BELGIAN WAFFLES

300 g (10½ oz) plain (all-purpose) flour
2½ tablespoons white sugar
3 tablespoons baking powder
1 teaspoon salt
2 eggs
435 ml (15 fl oz) warm milk
125 ml (4 fl oz) melted butter
1 teaspoon vanilla bean paste or extract

4 mini (60 g/2 oz) burratas
250 g (9 oz) blueberries
250 g (9 oz) strawberries, cut in half
20 g (¾ oz) coconut flakes
20 mint leaves
icing (confectioners') sugar, for dusting

MIXED BERRY SAUCE

300 g (10½ oz) frozen mixed berries
105 g (3½ oz) caster (superfine) sugar

SWEET RICOTTA

1 kg (2 lb 3 oz) traditional ricotta, drained
50 g (1¾ oz) caster (superfine) sugar
20 ml (¾ fl oz) olive oil

METHOD

To make the waffles, preheat the waffle iron.

Place the flour, sugar, baking powder and salt in a large bowl and whisk well to combine.

In a separate bowl, whisk the eggs, milk, melted butter and vanilla until well combined. Pour the wet ingredients into the dry and stir until just combined.

Pour some batter into the preheated waffle iron, following the manufacturer's instructions. Cook the waffles until golden brown. Repeat until all the batter has been used.

To make the mixed berry sauce, put the berries and sugar in a saucepan over a medium–high heat. Cook, stirring, until the sugar has dissolved, then set aside to cool. Once the mixture has cooled, pass it through a sieve.

For the sweet ricotta, combine all the ingredients in a blender and blitz until smooth.

TO SERVE Spread the sweet ricotta in a bowl, add the mixed berry sauce and swirl with a spatula to create a marble effect. Top with the mini burratas, fresh mixed berries, coconut flakes and mint. Serve with the hot waffles dusted with icing sugar.

SERVES 1

TOMATO & BURRATA CROISSANT

INGREDIENTS

10 cherry tomatoes on the vine
olive oil
1 croissant, cut lengthwise and toasted
1 × 90 g (3 oz) burrata
black pepper
5 basil leaves

METHOD

Preheat the oven to 200°C (390°F). Drizzle the tomatoes with olive oil and sprinkle with salt.

Roast the cherry tomatoes in the oven for 20 minutes, or until they start to blister.

TO SERVE Gently lay the tomatoes and croissant on a plate. Add the burrata on top of the croissant, season with salt and black pepper to taste, then scatter with basil leaves.

Alternatively, you can fill the croissant with the following combinations of ingredients:

- prosciutto, ricotta, honey
- smoked ham, rocket (arugula) and burrata
- salmon, chives, burrata

2

STARTERS

SERVES 4

BURRATA WITH BEETS

INGREDIENTS

2 large beetroot (beets)
black pepper
olive oil
fresh herbs such as thyme, to roast with the beetroot
1 quantity lemon dressing (see page 131)
4 × 90 g (3 oz) burratas
grapefruit segments, to serve
1 quantity herb oil (see page 95), to serve

BEETROOT RELISH

4 large red beetroot (beets), peeled
1 large granny smith apple, peeled and cored
20 g (¾ oz) ginger, finely chopped
60 g (2 oz) sugar
110 ml (4 fl oz) red wine vinegar

BEETROOT SALT

1 beetroot (beet)
salt

METHOD

Preheat the oven to 180°C (360°F). Season the two beetroot with salt, pepper, olive oil and your choice of herbs, wrap them in foil and bake for 50 minutes. Once cooked, peel the beetroot and cut into wedges.

To make the beetroot relish, grate the beetroot and apple together into a saucepan with a lid. Add all other relish ingredients, bring the mixture to a boil then cover, reduce the heat to low and cook for another 30 minutes, stirring from time to time.

After 30 minutes, remove the lid and cook for a further 10 minutes, until almost no liquid remains. Set aside to cool, then taste and adjust the seasoning as needed. It should taste sweet, but slightly sour.

To make the beetroot salt, preheat the oven to 70°C (160°F). Grate the whole beetroot, including the skin (but not the root) into a tray and cook for 1 hour, or until the mixture is completely dry. Once cool, weigh the beetroot and add the same weight in salt, then blend the mixture in a spice blender or coffee grinder.

TO SERVE Put the baked beetroot wedges in a bowl and season them with the lemon dressing, then set aside.

Take four plates and put a spoonful of the beetroot relish in the centre of each, then place a burrata on top. Scatter beetroot wedges and grapefruit segments around each plate. Season the burratas with the beetroot salt, then pool the herb oil around the relish.

SERVES 2

106 BURRATA WITH PROSCIUTTO, FIGS & VINO COTTO

INGREDIENTS

50 g (1¾ oz) rocket (arugula)
2 × 125 g (4½ oz) burratas
4 figs, cut into wedges
6 slices San Daniele prosciutto
1 tablespoon roasted walnuts, to garnish
black pepper

VINO COTTO DRESSING

20 ml (¾ fl oz) vino cotto
40 ml (1¼ fl oz) balsamic vinegar
60 ml (2 fl oz) olive oil

METHOD

To make the dressing, place the vino cotto, balsamic vinegar and salt in a bowl and whisk together. Once everything is well incorporated, add the olive oil slowly, whisking constantly, to emulsify.

TO ASSEMBLE Place the rocket in a bowl and dress with the vino cotto dressing, then transfer to a plate. Place the burratas on top of the rocket and arrange the fig wedges, prosciutto and walnuts around the plate. Season the burrata with salt, black pepper and the vino cotto dressing.

If figs are not in season you can substitute them with grilled peaches, roasted grapes, rockmelon or roasted peppers.

SERVES 2

108 FRIED BURRATA WITH ROMESCO SAUCE

INGREDIENTS

100 g (3½ oz) plain (all-purpose) flour
1 egg, whisked
100 g (3½ oz) breadcrumbs
2 mini (60 g/2 oz) burratas
vegetable oil, for frying
10 semi-dried tomatoes
10 basil leaves
½ tablespoon black sesame seeds
chilli oil
2 slices bread, grilled, to serve

ROMESCO SAUCE

450 g (1 lb) roasted red capsicums (bell peppers), skin and seeds removed
100 g (3½ oz) semi-dried tomatoes
pinch of salt
30 ml (1 fl oz) red wine vinegar
40 g (1½ oz) roasted almond flakes
50 ml (1¾ fl oz) olive oil

METHOD

To make the romesco sauce, place the roasted capsicums, semi-dried tomatoes, salt, vinegar and almond flakes in a blender and blitz. Add the olive oil and blend again until smooth.

To crumb the burratas, place the flour, egg and breadcrumbs into three separate bowls. Drain the burratas well and toss first in the flour, then in the egg, and lastly in the breadcrumbs (see overleaf). Shake off any excess breadcrumbs. Repeat this sequence once more, so the burrata is double crumbed.

Fry the crumbed burratas in hot oil for 2–3 minutes, until golden brown. Carefully remove with a slotted spoon to drain any excess oil.

TO SERVE Spoon the romesco sauce into the centre of a serving plate, then place the burratas on top. Scatter the semi-dried tomatoes, basil and black sesame seeds around the burratas, drizzle with chilli oil and season with salt. Serve with bread.

SERVES 2

112 TRUFFLE & ROCKET TOAST

INGREDIENTS

4 slices bread
olive oil
rocket (arugula)
2 mini (60 g/2 oz) burratas
black truffle, to garnish

TRUFFLE DRESSING

2 teaspoons truffle paste
2 teaspoons sherry vinegar
3 tablespoons olive oil

METHOD

Make the truffle dressing by combining the truffle paste, sherry vinegar and olive oil in a bowl. Whisk all the ingredients together and add salt to taste.

Brush each bread slice with olive oil and season with salt, then grill on a griddle pan for 2 minutes or until lightly toasted.

TO SERVE Take two plates, and place two slices of bread in the centre of each. Arrange some rocket around the bread, then place a burrata on top of the toast on each plate and drizzle the truffle dressing everywhere. Season the burratas with salt and shave some fresh truffle over the top.

TRUFFLE FACTS

Truffles are earthy treasures known for their intense aroma and deep flavour. These rare fungi grow underground and are challenging to harvest, often requiring specially trained dogs to sniff them out. While there are many species of truffle, the most common include:

- French black
- Italian white
- Summer truffle
- Bianchetto

Black truffles are typically milder in flavour and aroma, while white truffles are known for their strong, pungent fragrance. White truffles, most famously grown in Northern Italy, have a light-brown exterior with a tan or ivory interior. Black truffles, primarily cultivated in France, feature a brown-black exterior with a tan or brown interior.

Truffles are often shaved over or mixed into dishes like pasta, risotto, eggs, creamy soups, potatoes or chicken, or stirred into sauces for added depth and richness.

SERVES 4

SMOKY EGGPLANT, POLENTA CHIPS & BURRATA

INGREDIENTS

4 mini (60 g/2 oz) burratas
1 quantity herb oil (see page 95)
fennel fronds, to garnish
micro red cabbage (optional), to garnish

POLENTA CHIPS

250 ml (8½ oz) milk
250 ml (8½ oz) water
125 g (4½ oz) instant polenta (liquid measurements may change depending on the polenta you use)
15 g (½ oz) butter
40 g (1½ oz) Parmigiano Reggiano, grated
black pepper
olive oil, for frying
rice flour, for coating

SMOKY EGGPLANT PUREE

2 large eggplants (aubergine)
½ brown onion, julienned
¼ bunch flat-leaf (Italian) parsley, leaves picked and some of the stems roughly chopped
50 g (1¾ oz) tahini
200 g (7 oz) buffalo ricotta
20 ml (¾ fl oz) lemon juice

METHOD

To make the polenta chips, combine the milk and water in a small saucepan over a medium heat. Bring to the boil and then add the polenta. Stir until everything is well incorporated, then add the butter and Parmigiano Reggiano. Mix for around 2–3 minutes, until you obtain a silky and cheesy texture, then season to taste with salt and black pepper and immediately spread the polenta onto a tray lined with baking paper. You can use a spatula, a rolling pin or even your hand to do this – just be careful, as it will be very hot. Try to spread the polenta evenly to form a slab around 1 cm (½ in) thick.

Cover the polenta with another sheet of baking paper, then transfer to the fridge to cool completely. Once the slab is cold, turn it out onto a chopping board and cut into chips around 4–5 cm (1½–2 in) long.

To fry, heat a pot of oil to 170°C (340°F). While the oil is heating up, coat the chips in rice flour, working gently – they will be very fragile. Fry the chips in batches until they are golden, crispy and hot inside. Taste them, and season with salt if necessary.

To prepare the puree, cook the eggplants directly over a flame, burning the skin all over. Set them aside to cool, then peel and roughly chop them, and set aside.

In a saucepan with a splash of olive oil, saute the onion for 2 minutes, then add the eggplant and the parsley. Cook, stirring, until the onion is completely cooked and all the water from the eggplant has evaporated. Transfer the mixture to a blender, add the rest of the ingredients, then blend until smooth and season to taste. Keep the puree hot.

TO SERVE Spoon the eggplant puree onto four plates, then top with the burratas. Arrange the polenta chips around and drizzle the burratas with herb oil. Season the burratas with salt and black pepper, then garnish with fennel fronds and micro red cabbage, if using, and enjoy.

SERVES 2

ROASTED LEMON ZUCCHINI, CRISPY POTATOES & BURRATA

INGREDIENTS

1 × 90 g (3 oz) burrata
1 long red chilli, sliced into rounds
black sesame seeds, for sprinkling
snow pea (mangetout) tendrils, to garnish (optional)

ZUCCHINI PUREE

2 green zucchini, roughly chopped
½ brown onion, roughly chopped
20 g (¾ oz) spinach
25 g (1 oz) mint
25 g (1 oz) butter
black pepper

PAN-FRIED ZUCCHINI

1 medium green zucchini, cut into bite-sized rounds
olive oil
juice of ½ lemon

FRIED POTATOES

1 large chipper potato (use a starchy variety, such as russet)
vegetable oil, for frying

METHOD

To make the puree, add the zucchini and onion to a saucepan with a drizzle of olive oil and a pinch of salt. Cook over a low-medium heat until both ingredients are fully cooked and soft on the inside. Add the spinach, then sauté the ingredients together for 30 seconds, or until the spinach has wilted. Carefully transfer the hot mixture to a blender, making sure the lid is secure to prevent any splattering. Add the mint and the butter and blend until you have a smooth puree. If the puree is too thick, add a bit of water. Season with salt and pepper. If you are not using the puree immediately, refrigerate it, otherwise it will turn dark or start to oxidise.

To prepare the pan-fried zucchini, pan-fry the zucchini pieces with a little olive oil until they are almost fully cooked – they should still be a bit crunchy. Season with salt and pepper, then add the lemon juice at the very end.

Next, make the fried potatoes. Using a peeler, peel the potatoes into paper-thin strips.

Heat a pot of oil to 170°C (340°F). Fry the potatoes in batches unit they are golden and crispy, then drain on a paper towel to remove any excess oil. Sprinkle with salt.

TO SERVE Spoon the zucchini puree over a plate, then place the burrata in the centre of the puree. Arrange the fried zucchini and potatoes around the plate, then scatter with chilli rounds. Lastly, sprinkle black sesame seeds over the top and season the burrata with olive oil, salt and pepper. Garnish with snow pea tendrils, if using.

SERVES 1

TUNA TARTARE TORTILLA

INGREDIENTS

1 tortilla
1 mini (60 g/2 oz) burrata
salmon caviar, to garnish
micro herbs, to garnish
lime zest, to garnish

GUACAMOLE

1 avocado, ripe, skin and seed removed
olive oil
juice of 1 lime
black pepper

TUNA TARTARE

125 g (4½ oz) fresh tuna (sashimi grade), cut into 1 cm (½ in) dice
25 ml (¾ fl oz) ponzu sauce or soy sauce
½ teaspoon finely chopped shallots
½ teaspoon finely chopped red Thai chilli (optional)

METHOD

To make the guacamole, place the avocado in a mixing bowl and gently mash it with a fork. Add a drizzle of olive oil and lime juice and season to taste.

Next, prepare the tartare. Combine all the ingredients in a bowl, mix, then set aside to marinate for 5 minutes.

While the tartare is marinating, heat a splash of olive oil in a frying pan over a medium heat. Add the tortilla, frying until golden and crispy on both sides, then transfer to a plate lined with paper towel to absorb the oil. Set aside.

TO SERVE Spread the guacamole in the centre of the tortilla, then place the burrata on top. Arrange the tuna tartare around the burrata, reserving the juices. Sprinkle with salmon caviar and micro herbs, then season the burrata with olive oil, salt and lime zest. To finish, drizzle some of the tuna juices over the top.

SERVES 2–4

122 CROSTINI

INGREDIENTS

1 baguette, cut into 10 slices
10 baby (30 g/1 oz) burratas
10 whole anchovy fillets

ROASTED GRAPES

500 g (1 lb 2 oz) seedless black grapes
3 sprigs fresh thyme
4 teaspoons fresh thyme leaves
4 tablespoons olive oil
cracked black pepper

SALSA VERDE

1–2 garlic cloves, minced
2 anchovy fillets, drained and roughly chopped
handful fresh flat-leaf (Italian) parsley leaves, finely chopped
handful fresh coriander (cilantro) leaves, finely chopped
handful spinach leaves
handful mint leaves
100 ml (3½ fl oz) extra-virgin olive oil
zest of 1 lemon

METHOD

Preheat the oven to 180°C (360°F). Arrange the sliced baguette on a lined baking tray. Brush with a little olive oil and bake for 10 minutes, until golden. Remove and set aside to completely cool. Leave the oven on to roast the grapes.

Arrange the grapes on a baking tray. Add the fresh thyme sprigs and leaves, drizzle with olive oil and season well with salt and pepper. Gently toss to coat, then bake in the oven for 20–25 minutes until they are blistered and jammy.

To make the salsa verde, combine all the ingredients and some salt and pepper in a food processor and blitz until smooth. Set aside.

TO SERVE Arrange the toasted baguette slices on a large serving platter. Top some with one baby burrrata, a spoonful of salsa verde and and an anchovy fillet and some with roasted grapes and burrata.

Garnish with a drizzle of olive oil.

SERVES 4–6

ANTIPASTO PLATTER

INGREDIENTS

mix of baby burrata and burrata
mixed cured meats such as prosciutto, hot salami and capocollo, thinly sliced
1 baguette, sliced

MIXED MARINATED OLIVES

150 g (5½ oz) Sicilian olives
100 g (3½ oz) green Spanish olives
100 g (3½ oz) kalamata olives
6 garlic cloves, peeled and thinly sliced
rind of 1 lemon
rind of 1 orange
fresh chilli, thinly sliced
375 ml (12½ fl oz) extra-virgin olive oil
fresh thyme, rosemary and oregano leaves

GRILLED MIXED VEGETABLES

2 × zucchini, thinly sliced lengthways
2 × red capsicums (bell peppers), stem and seeds removed, sliced into strips
2 garlic cloves, peeled and finely sliced
125 ml (4 fl oz) extra-virgin olive oil
black pepper
fresh basil leaves, to garnish

MIXED TOMATOES

200 g (7 oz) mixed tomatoes such as roma (plum), heirloom and cherry
60 ml (2 fl oz) extra-virgin olive oil
handful fresh basil leaves, roughly chopped

METHOD

To make the mixed marinated olives, combine all the ingredients in a saucepan and gently warm over a low heat for 5 minutes. Serve warm in a bowl.

Next, prepare the grilled vegetables. Heat a grill pan over a medium heat. Add the zucchini and capsicums and grill for 4–5 minutes, until soft and charred. Transfer to a bowl with the garlic and olive oil and season with salt and pepper. Toss to combine, then scatter basil leaves over the top.

To make the mixed tomatoes, dice the tomatoes into bite-sized pieces and put in a bowl. Season well with extra-virgin olive oil and salt, then scatter the basil leaves over. Stir and set aside.

TO ASSEMBLE Arrange the burratas on a large cheese board. Arrange the bowl of olives, grilled vegetables, mixed tomatoes, cured meats and sliced baguette around the burrata and serve.

3

MAINS

MAKES 6 PORTIONS

BASIL PESTO

INGREDIENTS

90 g (3 oz) basil leaves
30 g (1 oz) baby spinach
2 teaspoons pine nuts, lightly toasted
200 ml (7 fl oz) olive oil
3 strips of lemon peel, pith removed
75 g (2¾ oz) Grana Padano, grated

METHOD

Blanch the basil and spinach in a large saucepan of boiling water, then refresh in iced water. Pat dry using a tea towel (dish towel). Add to a blender along with the pine nuts, olive oil, lemon peel and a pinch of salt and blend until completely smooth. Transfer to a bowl, then add the Grana Padano and mix with a spatula to combine.

Alternatively, a mortar and pestle is another option you could use to achieve this for a more rustic feel.

MAKES 1 PORTION

LEMON DRESSING

INGREDIENTS

150 ml (5 fl oz) lemon juice
1 tablespoon honey
1 teaspoon salt
1 tablespoon dijon mustard
150 ml (5 fl oz) olive oil

METHOD

Mix all ingredients in a bowl except for the oil. Whisk until everything is well incorporated, then add the oil slowly, while whisking, until the mixture has emulsified.

SERVES 2

BURRATA, CAULIFLOWER PUREE & GRILLED ASPARAGUS

INGREDIENTS

2 × 125 g (4½ oz) burratas
6 asparagus spears, grilled
olive oil

ROCKET PESTO

30 g (1 oz) rocket (arugula), leaves only
100 g (3½ oz) baby spinach
1 tablespoon walnuts, lightly toasted
60 ml (2 fl oz) olive oil
peel of 2 lemons, pith removed
30 g (1 oz) Grana Padano, grated

CAULIFLOWER PUREE

½ cauliflower
1 green Thai chilli, whole
milk, to cover
water, to cover
100 g (3½ oz) unsalted butter

CRISPY QUINOA

30 g (1 oz) quinoa
250 ml (8½ fl oz) vegetable oil, for frying

METHOD

To make the rocket pesto, bring a large saucepan of water to the boil. Once boiling, blanch the rocket and spinach, then refresh in iced water. Pat dry using a tea towel (dish towel). Add to a blender along with the walnuts, olive oil, lemon peel and a pinch of salt, and blend until completely smooth. Transfer to a bowl, then add the Grana Padano and mix with a spatula. Set aside. Alternatively, you can use basil pesto (see page 131).

Next, prepare the cauliflower puree. Cut the cauliflower into florets and place them in a medium saucepan. Add the chilli and cover with equal parts milk and water. Simmer for 10 minutes, until the cauliflower is completely cooked, then strain, reserving the liquid. Put the cauliflower in a blender, then add the butter and blend until smooth. If the puree is dry, add some of the reserved cooking liquid. Season to taste with salt, then set aside and keep warm.

Fill a medium saucepan with water and bring to the boil. Add the quinoa and a pinch of salt and simmer for 15 minutes. Drain, and spread the quinoa on a tray lined with baking paper, then refrigerate for a couple of hours to let it dry.

Fill a saucepan with enough oil to deep-fry and bring it to 180°C (360°F). While the oil is heating up, separate the quinoa with your hands so it is as loose as possible. Fry the quinoa, mixing with tongs until the quinoa is golden and crispy. Drain on a plate lined with paper towel and season to taste with salt.

TO SERVE Spoon the cauliflower puree over two plates, then place a burrata in the middle of each. Spoon the pesto around the puree, then top with the asparagus spears. Season the burratas with salt and olive oil, then sprinkle the quinoa all over the plates.

SERVES 2

134 BURRATA IN CROSTA

INGREDIENTS

1 × 90 g (3 oz) burrata
1 sheet puff pastry
black pepper
8 slices prosciutto
4 kalamata olives, pitted and sliced into rounds
1 egg, whisked
1 quantity basil pesto (see page 131)
basil leaves, to garnish
100 g (3½ oz) heirloom tomatoes, halved and seasoned with olive oil, salt and black pepper

BEURRE FONDUE

110 ml (4 fl oz) water
1 teaspoon salt
340 g (12 oz) butter, cubed

METHOD

Preheat the oven to 180°C (360°F).

Cut the knot off the burrata. Lay the puff pastry on the bench, top with two slices of prosciutto, then place the burrata in the middle and season with salt and pepper. Add the olives and close the puff pastry, forming a bag around the burrata. Trim off the excess pastry then, using a pastry brush, coat the pastry parcel with the egg (see overleaf). Cook for 12–15 minutes, or until the puff pastry is puffed up and golden.

Next, make the beurre fondue. Put the water, salt and 250 g (9 oz) of the butter in a saucepan over a medium-high heat. When the butter is almost melted, take off the heat and add the rest of the butter. Using a hand blender, emulsify everything together (blend until all the butter is completely melted and you have a creamy sauce – the colour of the sauce should be a pale yellow). Keep the sauce in a warm place or a bain-marie. If the sauce gets cold, it will split.

Combine the beurre fondue and the basil pesto in a small saucepan over a medium heat. Whisk until the mixture is warm, being careful not to let it boil or the sauce will split.

TO SERVE Place the burrata parcel in the middle of a plate, then arrange the basil leaves, tomatoes and remaining prosciutto around it. To finish, drizzle the creamy basil sauce over the top.

SERVES 4

138 BARLEY, MUSHROOMS & BURRATA

INGREDIENTS

800 ml (27 fl oz) water or stock (if using water, add salt)
250 g (9 oz) pearl barley
600 g (1lb 5 oz) mixed mushrooms (portobello, pearl and king oyster, cut into bite-sized pieces)
40 g (1½ oz) pancetta, diced
120 ml (4 fl oz) white wine
50 g (1¾ oz) butter
4 × 90 g (3 oz) burratas
black pepper
dill and mint, to garnish
chilli oil, for drizzling

HERB BUTTER

80 g (2¾ oz) butter, softened
35 g (1¼ oz) mixed herbs (thyme, sage, mint), roughly chopped

METHOD

To make the herb butter, mix the butter and chopped herbs together until well combined. Set aside.

Bring the water or stock to a boil in a medium saucepan, then add the barley and simmer for 25 minutes, until the barley is fully cooked. Remove from the heat, add the herb butter and stir through, then season with salt to taste. Keep warm.

Warm a drizzle of oil in a large saucepan, then add the mixed mushrooms and the pancetta. Cook over a high heat until everything is caramelised and golden – approximately 4 minutes. Deglaze with the wine, continue cooking for 5 minutes, then lower the temperature and add the butter to glaze the mushrooms. Season to taste with salt, then serve immediately.

TO SERVE Put the barley in a bowl, then place the burrata in the middle. Season with salt and pepper, then spoon the mushrooms over the barley. Garnish with mint and dill, then drizzle everything with chilli oil.

SERVES 4

BEETROOT SOUP

INGREDIENTS

olive oil
1 large potato, diced
4 large beetroot (beets), cut into 5 mm (¼ in) dice
1 brown onion, julienned
20 g (¾ oz) ground cumin
100 g (3½ oz) butter
black pepper
4 mini (60 g/2 oz) burratas
croutons, to serve
4 sprigs coriander (cilantro), leaves picked, to garnish
crusty bread, to serve

BEETROOT DICE

1 medium beetroot, diced into 1 cm (½ in) cubes
15 g (½ oz) unsalted butter

METHOD

To make the beetroot, boil the cubed beetroot in water for 5–7 minutes, until firm but soft in the centre. Drain, then transfer the beetroot to a pan with the butter and 30 ml (1 fl oz) water. Season with salt and warm in a small pan over a medium heat for 1 minute, until the beetroot is glazed with the butter, then set aside.

To make the soup, warm a drizzle of olive oil in a large saucepan over a medium heat, then add the potato, beetroot and onion. Cook for 5 minutes, stirring constantly, then add the cumin and cook for another 5 minutes. Add enough water to cover all the ingredients and simmer for 30 minutes, or until the beetroot and potatoes are fully cooked.

Pass through a sieve, reserving the liquid. Place the cooked vegetables in a blender, add the butter and blitz, adding cooking liquid as needed to obtain a creamy soup. Season with salt and black pepper to taste.

TO SERVE Pour the soup into four soup bowls, then top each with a burrata, croutons and some of the beetroot dice. Season the burrata with salt, olive oil and black pepper and garnish with coriander leaves. Serve with crusty bread.

SERVES 4

142 PEAS, FENNEL & ORANGE BURRATA

INGREDIENTS

4 × 125 g (4½ oz) burratas
40 g (1½ oz) peas, blanched
16 sugar-snap peas, blanched and cut in half
1 bulb fennel, shaved
20 orange segments

PARSLEY BREADCRUMBS

80 g (2¾ oz) breadcrumbs
50 g (1¾ oz) flat-leaf (Italian) parsley
½ teaspoon salt

PEA PUREE

1 shallot, julienned
4 black peppercorns
4 sprigs thyme
400 g (14 oz) peas
100 ml (3½ fl oz) white wine
50 g (1¾ oz) spinach
40 g (1½ oz) butter

ORANGE DRESSING

80 ml (2½ fl oz) orange juice
65 ml (2¼ fl oz) lemon juice
1 teaspoon salt
150 ml (5 fl oz) olive oil
black pepper
1 tablespoon honey
1 tablespoon dijon mustard

METHOD

To make the parsley breadcrumbs, mix all the ingredients in a blender until everything is well combined. Refrigerate until ready to serve.

Next, make the pea puree. Warm a drizzle of olive oil in a medium saucepan. Sauté the shallot, peppercorns and thyme for 3 minutes, then add the peas. Cook for a couple of minutes, then deglaze with white wine. Add enough water to cover the peas and simmer for 15 minutes, or until the peas are fully cooked. Add the spinach at the end and remove from the heat as soon as it is cooked. Pass the mixture through a sieve, reserving the liquid.

Put the pea mixture in a blender, add the butter and blend until smooth. Add some of the cooking water to loosen the puree if needed, then set aside to cool.

To make the orange dressing, mix all the ingredients together, then set aside. Alternatively, you can also use the lemon dressing on page 131.

TO SERVE Spoon the pea puree onto four plates, then place a burrata on top of each. In a bowl, mix the peas, sugar-snap peas, fennel and orange segments, then pour the orange dressing over and toss. Arrange the salad around the burratas, then scatter the parsley breadcrumbs over the entire dish.

SERVES 4

BURRATA WITH ROCKMELON, PROSCIUTTO & CUCUMBER

INGREDIENTS

½ cucumber
24 slices prosciutto
olive oil
4 × 125 g (4½ oz) burratas
20 rockmelon slices
black pepper

ROCKMELON GEL

1 medium rockmelon
lemon juice
sugar
agar agar

METHOD

To prepare the cucumber, remove the seeds, then slice with a peeler lengthwise. Reserve the cucumber ribbons in iced water so they curl.

Next, make the rockmelon gel. Peel the melon, remove the seeds and blend to a liquid. Filter the melon juice using a sieve lined with a coffee filter. Don't push it, let it filter on its own. Taste the liquid and add a couple of drops of lemon juice and sugar if the melon is not sweet or the flavour is bland. Weigh the liquid, and for every 100 ml (3½ fl oz) of melon juice add 1 g (1/32 oz) of agar agar. Transfer the mixture to a saucepan and whisk constantly over a medium heat until it boils. Remove from the heat and pour into a bowl. Rest the bowl over a bowl filled with ice and water – this will cool it down and help to ensure a bright colour. Once the mixture has cooled to form a gel, blend it again until smooth. Transfer to a piping bag or a squeeze bottle and set aside.

Preheat the oven to 180°C (360°F). Lay 12 of the prosciutto slices on an oven tray lined with baking paper, then cover with another piece of baking paper and top with another tray. Bake the prosciutto for approximately 12 minutes, or until golden and crispy. Remove from the oven and transfer to a tray lined with paper towel to drain.

TO SERVE Drain the cucumber ribbons, then season with salt and olive oil. Squeeze a dot of melon gel in the centre of a plate, then put a burrata on top. Arrange the prosciutto, crispy prosciutto, rockmelon slices and cucumber ribbons around the burrata. To finish, season the burrata with olive oil, salt and pepper and dot melon gel around the plate.

SERVES 4

146 BUTTERNUT PUMPKIN SOUP

INGREDIENTS

200 g (7 oz) butternut pumpkin (winter squash), cut into 7 mm (3/8 in) dice
30 g (1 oz) unsalted butter
4 × 90 g (3 oz) burratas
olive oil
black pepper
chopped chives, to garnish

PUMPKIN SOUP

1.3 kg (2 lb 14 oz) butternut pumpkin (winter squash), roughly chopped
150 g (5½ oz) butter
black pepper

METHOD

Blanch the diced pumpkin in boiling water until soft. Drain, then glaze with the butter. Set aside.

To make the soup, put the chopped pumpkin into a large saucepan and cover with water. Bring to the boil over a medium heat, then simmer until the pumpkin is soft. Remove from the heat and drain, reserving the cooking water. Put the pumpkin in a blender, add the butter and blend. Slowly add some of the cooking water until you obtain a soup texture. Season with black pepper and salt.

TO SERVE Put some of the diced pumpkin in the bottom of each of four soup bowls, then place the burratas on top and season with olive oil, salt and black pepper. Pour the soup over and garnish with the chives.

SERVES 2

148 GAZPACHO

INGREDIENTS

2 mini (60 g/2 oz) burratas
raspberries, halved, to garnish
purple basil leaves, to garnish
1 long red chilli, sliced into rounds, to garnish
black pepper

GAZPACHO

10 basil leaves
35 ml (1¼ fl oz) olive oil
350 g (12½ oz) cherry tomatoes
150 g (5½ oz) raspberries
½ shallot, diced
15 red capsicums (bell peppers), skin and seeds removed
15 cucumbers, skin and seeds removed
40 g (1½ oz) bread
50 g (1¾ oz) ice
2 tablespoons red wine vinegar
black pepper

BASIL OIL

100 ml (3½ fl oz) olive oil
2 tablespoons basil leaves
½ teaspoon salt

BAKED TOMATOES

5 heirloom tomatoes, halved
black pepper
olive oil

METHOD

To make the gazpacho, place all the ingredients in a blender and blend until smooth. Add salt and pepper to taste, then refrigerate until serving.

For the basil oil, blend all the ingredients together until smooth. Transfer to a small saucepan, warm to 60°C (140°F), then cook for 1 minute.

Strain the oil through a fine chinois or sieve, then transfer to a bowl.

To bake the tomatoes, preheat the oven to 170°C (340°F). Put the tomatoes in a bowl and season with salt, black pepper and olive oil. Mix gently, then arrange on a tray lined with baking paper. Cook for 40 minutes to 1 hour – they should be cooked, but not a puree.

TO SERVE Pour the gazpacho into two soup bowls. Top each bowl with a burrata, then spoon the raspberries, baked tomatoes, basil and chilli over the top. Season the burrata with salt and black pepper and drizzle with basil oil.

SERVES 4

CRISPY CHEESY POLENTA & BURRATA

INGREDIENTS

4 × 125 g (4½ oz) burratas
12 slices smoked salmon
1 quantity lemon dressing (see page 131)

PICKLED FENNEL

100 ml (3½ fl oz) water
100 ml (3½ fl oz) white vinegar
1 star anise
3 black peppercorns
70 g (2½ oz) white sugar
1 large fennel

CHEESY POLENTA

250 ml (8½ fl oz) milk
250 ml (8½ fl oz) water
125 g (4½ oz) instant polenta (liquid measurements may change depending on the polenta you use)
15 g (½ oz) butter
40 g (1½ oz) parmesan cheese
black pepper
250 ml (8½ oz) vegetable oil, for frying

TO CRUMB

100 g (3½ oz) plain (all-purpose) flour
1 egg, whisked
100 g (3½ oz) breadcrumbs

HERB RICOTTA

500 g (1 lb 2 oz) ricotta
1 tablespoon mixed herbs (mint, sage, rosemary, thyme, flat-leaf (Italian) parsley)
2 teaspoons salt
1 teaspoon lemon juice
2 teaspoons water

CONTINUED OVERLEAF

The day before, prepare the pickled fennel by placing all the ingredients except the fennel in a small saucepan. Bring to the boil, then turn off the heat, cover with a lid and let the mixture infuse for another 5 minutes. Strain the liquid.

Meanwhile, thinly slice the fennel. Mix the fennel and pickling liquid in a vacuum pack if possible, otherwise mix in a container, making sure the fennel is completely submerged in the liquid.

Combine the milk and water in a small saucepan over a medium heat. Bring to the boil and then add the polenta. Stir until everything is well incorporated, then add the butter and parmesan. Mix for around 2–3 minutes, until you obtain a silky and cheesy texture, then season to taste with salt and black pepper and immediately spread the polenta onto a tray lined with baking paper. You can use a spatula, a rolling pin or even your hand to do this – just be careful, as it will be very hot. Try to spread the polenta evenly to form a slab around 1 cm (½ in) thick.

Cover the polenta with another sheet of baking paper, then transfer to the fridge to cool completely. Once the slab is cold, turn it out onto a chopping board and cut into rectangles 12 × 7 cm (4¾ × 2¾ in).

To crumb the burratas, place the flour, egg and breadcrumbs into three separate bowls. Drain the burratas well and toss first in the flour, then in the egg, and lastly in the breadcrumbs. Shake off any excess breadcrumbs. Repeat this sequence once more, so the burrata is double crumbed.

Preheat the oven to 180°C (360°F). Put the oil in a saucepan and heat to 170°C (340°F), then fry the polenta rectangles until they are golden and crispy. Finish in the oven for 5 minutes, then set aside.

Next, make the herb ricotta. Combine all the ingredients in a blender and blitz until smooth.

TO ASSEMBLE Place the polenta on a plate, then spread with a layer of herb ricotta. Top with the pickled fennel, add a burrata and arrange the smoked salmon around. Season the burrata with salt and black pepper, then drizzle the lemon dressing over the burrata and around the plate.

SERVES 4

PEA SOUP & CRISPY PANCETTA

INGREDIENTS

40 g (1½ oz) peas
30 g (1 oz) butter
3 slices pancetta
4 mini (60 g/2 oz) burratas
10 mint leaves, to garnish
olive oil
black pepper

PEA SOUP

½ onion, julienned
3 sprigs thyme
400 g (14 oz) peas
80 g (2¾ oz) spinach
1 tablespoon mint leaves
50 g (1¾ oz) butter
black pepper

METHOD

Blanch the peas, then drain, glaze with butter and a little water and season with salt. Set aside until ready to serve.

Preheat the oven to 180°C (360°F). Lay the pancetta on a tray lined with baking paper, then cover with another sheet of baking paper and top with another tray. Bake the pancetta for 10–12 minutes. Let it cool, then roughly chop it.

To make the pea soup, heat a drizzle of olive oil in a medium saucepan, then add the onion and thyme and cook for 3 minutes. Add the peas and cook for a further 5 minutes, then add enough water to cover everything. Bring it to the boil and simmer until the peas are tender. Add the spinach and mint and cook for 1 more minute. Cool slightly, then transfer the mixture to a blender. Add the butter and blend, adding water as needed until you achieve a nice smooth consistency. Season with salt and black pepper.

TO SERVE Pour the soup into a bowl. Top with the burrata, and season the burrata with olive oil, salt and pepper. Sprinkle the peas and crispy pancetta over the top, then garnish with mint.

SERVES 4

156 RISOTTO VERDE WITH SCALLOPS

INGREDIENTS

12 scallops
4 mini (60 g/2 oz) burratas
1 quantity baked tomatoes (see page 148)
olive oil
lime zest, to garnish

ROCKET PESTO

30 g (1 oz) rocket (arugula), leaves only
100 g (3½ oz) baby spinach
1 tablespoon walnuts, lightly toasted
60 ml (2 fl oz) olive oil
peel of 2 lemons, pith removed
30 g (1 oz) Grana Padano, grated

RISOTTO

900 ml (30½ fl oz) vegetable stock
290 g (10 oz) risotto rice
50 ml (1¾ fl oz) white wine
30 g (1 oz) butter

METHOD

To make the rocket pesto, bring a large saucepan of water to the boil. Once boiling, blanch the rocket and spinach, then refresh in iced water. Pat dry using a tea towel (dish towel). Add to a blender along with the walnuts, olive oil, lemon peel and a pinch of salt, and blend until completely smooth. Transfer to a bowl, then add the Grana Padano and mix with a spatula. Set aside.

To make the risotto, warm the stock in a saucepan over a medium heat. In another saucepan, add the rice and toast over a medium heat for 1 minute, then deglaze with wine. Add the stock a little at a time, stirring constantly, for around 15 minutes, until all the liquid has been absorbed and the rice is tender. Add the pesto and butter, stir through, and season with salt.

Just before you are ready to serve, grill the scallops. Heat a grill pan on the stove, then sear the scallops for 3–5 minutes, turning them halfway through cooking. Season with salt, then plate immediately.

TO SERVE Spoon the risotto onto four plates and top each with a burrata. Arrange the scallops and baked tomatoes around the risotto, then season the burrata with olive oil, salt and a little lime zest.

SERVES 6

158 ZUCCHINI, PANCETTA & LEEK TART

INGREDIENTS

- 1 sheet puff pastry
- 300 g (10½ oz) pancetta, roughly diced
- 3 zucchini, thinly sliced
- 3 leeks, green stem removed and thinly sliced
- 1 tablespoon white wine
- 3 eggs, whisked
- 100 ml (3½ fl oz) pouring (single/light) cream
- black pepper
- 4 mini (60 g/2 oz) burratas

METHOD

Preheat the oven to 180°C (360°F) and line an 18 cm (7 in) round tart tin with the puff pastry. Press down to ensure the tin is completely covered.

In a frying pan over a medium heat, fry the pancetta for 6–8 minutes, until crispy. Remove the pancetta with a slotted spoon and set aside. In the same pan, fry off the zucchini (reserve 1 cup for garnish) and the leek for about 10 minutes, until soft.

Return the pancetta to the pan with the zucchini and leek and stir to combine. Deglaze with white wine and fry for 1–2 minutes to cook off the alcohol, stirring to make sure the ingredients are well combined. Turn off the heat and allow the mixture to cool completely.

Once cooled, add the eggs and cream. Season well with salt and pepper and stir to combine. Pour the mixture carefully into the prepared tart case and spread with a spatula to ensure the mixture is even. Arrange the reserved zucchini over the top in a circular pattern.

Bake in the oven for 20 minutes, until the tart has set and is golden on the top.

Season with black pepper and drizzle with olive oil, then top with burratas and serve.

SERVES 4

PURÈ DI FAVE, GRILLED OCTOPUS & CICORIA

INGREDIENTS

250 g (9 oz) dried broad beans
olive oil
black pepper
1 bunch chicory (endive), rinsed, stems removed and roughly chopped
1 garlic clove, minced
1 teaspoon red pepper flakes
100 ml (3½ fl oz) olive oil
450 g (1 lb) baby octopus, beak and eyes removed (ask your fishmonger to do this for you)
1 tablespoon lemon juice
4 × 30 g (1 oz) baby burratas
chilli flakes, to garnish

METHOD

Soak the broad beans in water for 6 hours or overnight, to soften, then drain and rinse well. Once the beans are soft, peel off the skins and discard.

Transfer the beans to a saucepan and cover with water. Bring to the boil, then reduce the heat to medium and cook for 40–45 minutes, until the beans are tender. Drain, then transfer to a food processor. Season well with olive oil, salt and pepper and blitz until you have a smooth puree. Place in a serving bowl and set aside.

Add the chicory to a frying pan along with the garlic, red pepper flakes and olive oil and cook over a medium–low heat for 3–4 minutes, until the chicory is soft and tender. Remove from the heat and set aside.

To cook the baby octopus, bring a pot of water to the boil, then add the baby octopus along with the lemon juice. Reduce the heat and simmer for 25–30 minutes, until tender. Drain well.

Drizzle the octopus with olive oil, and season with salt and pepper. Heat a grill pan over high heat and cook the octopus for 3–4 minutes each side, until charred.

TO ASSEMBLE Spoon the broad bean puree onto a large serving platter, then top with the grilled baby octopus, chicory and burratas. Finish with a sprinkle of chilli flakes and black pepper.

MAKES 6 × 250 G (9 OZ) DOUGH BALLS

NEAPOLITAN-STYLE PIZZA DOUGH

By guest Chef Salim Gafayri

INGREDIENTS

600 ml (20½ fl oz) cold tap water
½ teaspoon dry yeast
1 kg (2 lb 3 oz) 00 flour
30 g (1 oz) Italian fine sea salt
fine semolina, for dusting

METHOD

Pour the water into a large mixing bowl and add the yeast, stirring to dissolve. Add 500 g (1 lb 2 oz) of the flour to the bowl and mix with your hands for 30 seconds to combine.

Add the remaining flour to the bowl and mix for another 30 seconds to combine, then add the salt and mix for a further 30 seconds.

Tip the dough mass onto your benchtop and knead with your hands for 10 minutes.

Shape the dough mass into a smooth ball by dragging it across the benchtop to form tension on the outside of the dough. Cover and leave the dough to rest in the fridge for 24 hours.

After the dough has rested, portion the dough into 250 g (9 oz) pieces. Shape each piece into a ball, then rest for 10–12 hours in an airtight container. The dough will keep in the fridge for roughly 24–48 hours, but it's best to use it immediately.

Take the dough out of the fridge 1½ hours before cooking (1 hour if the weather is hot). The dough temperature should be between 16–18°C (60–65°F).

Use fine semolina to stretch your dough. Flour your hands and gently open your pizza ball, pressing with the middle three fingers on each hand to open it up. Using your palms, stretch and rotate the base to the required size.

Enjoy your authentic Neapolitan-style pizza!

MAKES 1 PIZZA

BURRATA PIZZA WITH CAPONATA

By guest Chef Salim Gafayri

INGREDIENTS

- 1 × 250 g (9 oz) ball Neapolitan-style pizza dough (see page 165)
- fine semolina
- 100 g (3½ oz) fior di latte
- 1 × 125 g (4½ oz) burrata
- flat-leaf (Italian) parsley leaves, olive oil and chilli flakes (optional), to garnish

CAPONATA MIX

- 5 tablespoons olive oil
- 2 kg (4 lb 6 oz) eggplant (aubergine), unpeeled, cut into 1 cm (½ in) cubes
- 1 medium onion, cubed
- 4 large garlic cloves, chopped
- 1 × 400 g (14 oz) tin diced tomatoes
- 3 tablespoons red wine vinegar
- 2 tablespoons drained capers
- black pepper
- 20 g (¾ oz) chopped fresh basil leaves
- handful toasted pine nuts

METHOD

To make the caponata, mix heat the oil in large, heavy-based saucepan over a medium heat.

Add the eggplant, onion and garlic. Sauté for about 15 minutes, until the eggplant is soft and brown. Add the diced tomatoes, red wine vinegar and capers, then cover and simmer, stirring occasionally, for 12 minutes, until the eggplant and onion are very tender.

Season to taste with salt and pepper, then mix in the fresh basil.

Preheat oven to 250°C (480°F).

Place your pizza dough in the fine semolina and stretch into a circle around 28–30 cm (11–12 in). Transfer to a baking tray or pizza stone, then spread the cold caponata mix on the base, and scatter with hand-torn fior di latte.

Bake the pizza for 8–10 minutes, or until the base is golden.

Garnish with the burrata, parsley and olive oil, and chilli flakes, if using.

MAKES 1 PIZZA

BURRATA PIZZA WITH VODKA SAUCE

By guest Chef Salim Gafayri

INGREDIENTS

1 × 250 g (9 oz) ball Neapolitan-style pizza dough (see page 165)
fine semolina
80 g (2¾ oz) fior di latte
1 × 125 g (4½ oz) burrata
purple or green basil leaves, to garnish

VODKA SAUCE

200 ml (7 fl oz) olive oil
120 g (4½ oz) brown onions, finely chopped
1 teaspoon crushed garlic
120 ml (4 fl oz) vodka
500 g (1 lb 2 oz) crushed tomatoes
120 ml (4 fl oz) thick (double/heavy) cream
100 g (3½ oz) parmesan cheese, grated
1 tablespoon Italian fine sea salt
1 teaspoon cracked black pepper

METHOD

To make the vodka sauce, warm the olive oil in a saucepan over a medium heat.

Add the onions and garlic and gently sauté until they are translucent, without colouring.

Deglaze the pan with the vodka and cook for about 2 minutes, until the alcohol has evaporated.

Add the crushed tomatoes and cook over a low heat for 10 minutes.

Add the cream, salt and pepper and simmer for 5 minutes, then set aside to cool.

Using a hand blender, blend the sauce until it reaches a smooth consistency.

Add the parmesan cheese and stir.

Return the sauce to the pan and cook down for another 5 minutes, until it thickens. Once cooled, you can use the sauce on your pizza. Alternatively, serve it warm as a crust dipper.

Preheat oven to 250°C (480°F).

Place your pizza dough in the fine semolina and stretch into a circle around 28–30 cm (11–12 in). Transfer to a baking tray or pizza stone, then spread 100 g (3½ oz) of the cold vodka sauce on the base, and scatter with hand-torn fior di latte.

Bake the pizza for 8–10 minutes, or until the base is golden.

Garnish with burrata and basil leaves.

MAKES 1 PIZZA

BURRATA PIZZA WITH ZUCCHINI FLOWERS

By guest Chef Salim Gafayri

INGREDIENTS

2 × zucchini flowers
1 × 250 g (9 oz) ball Neapolitan-style pizza dough (see page 165)
fine semolina
100 g (3½ oz) fior di latte
olive oil
20 g (¾ oz) parmesan cheese, grated
1 × 125 g (4½ oz) burrata
zest of ½ lemon, to garnish
black pepper

METHOD

Preheat oven to 250°C (480°F).

Clean the zucchini flowers and separate the flower leaves gently. Heat a grill pan on the stove. Lightly grill the stem of the zucchini flower for 90 seconds on each side, then slice it in half.

Place your pizza dough in the fine semolina and stretch into a circle around 28–30 cm (11–12 in). Transfer to a baking tray or pizza stone. Scatter with hand-torn fior di latte, then spread the zucchini flowers and stems over. Drizzle with olive oil and season with a pinch of salt.

Bake the pizza for 8–10 minutes, or until the base is golden.

Garnish with parmesan, burrata and lemon zest, olive oil and black pepper.

4

PASTA

SERVES 4

SPAGHETTI ALLA AMATRICIANA WITH CACIOTTA

INGREDIENTS

400 g (14 oz) spaghetti
70 g (2½ oz) guanciale, diced
1 long red chilli, sliced into rounds
4 wheels plain caciotta, at room temperature
2 mini (60 g/2 oz) burratas
black pepper
olive oil

NAPOLI SAUCE

50 ml (1¾ fl oz) olive oil
½ brown onion, roughly chopped
½ carrot, roughly chopped
1 kg (2 lb 3 oz) whole peeled tomatoes
handful basil leaves
1 teaspoon salt
1 teaspoon sugar

METHOD

To make the napoli sauce, warm the olive oil in a medium saucepan over a low heat, then sauté the onion and carrot for 5 minutes, stirring from time to time. Add the tomatoes and cook gently over a low heat until the tomatoes dissolve in the sauce (around 40 minutes to 1 hour). Once the tomatoes are cooked, add the basil, salt and sugar then blend with a hand blender or in a regular blender.

Bring a large pot of water to the boil. Add the spaghetti and cook according to the instructions on the packet, until al dente. While the pasta is cooking, fry the guanciale in a frying pan over a low heat, allowing the fat to render. When the guanciale is crispy, add the chilli and cook for 1 minute, then add the napoli sauce. Once the pasta is cooked, drain and toss through the sauce. Season to taste with salt.

TO SERVE Place each caciotta in the middle of a plate. Using a spoon, carve out some of the inside of each caciotta, creating a hollow for the pasta to sit in. Using tongs, nest some of the spaghetti in each caciotta hollow, then spoon some of the sauce and guanciale over the top. Place a burrata in the top of the nest and season with olive oil, salt and black pepper.

SERVES 4

178 GNOCCHI WITH CACIOCAVALLO LEMON SAUCE & BASIL PESTO

INGREDIENTS

400 g (14 oz) gnocchi
4 × 90 g (3 oz) burratas
1½ tablespoons pine nuts
1 quantity basil pesto (see page 131)
purple and green basil leaves

BASIL SALT

basil leaves (no stems)
4 g (⅛ oz) salt

CACIOCAVALLO LEMON SAUCE

450 g (1 lb) butter
90 ml (3 fl oz) lemon juice
5 g (⅛ oz) salt
60 ml (2 fl oz) water
125 g (4½ oz) caciocavallo, grated

METHOD

To make the basil salt, first dehydrate the basil leaves. Line a flat plate with paper towel, then spread the basil leaves on the plate, ensuring they don't overlap. Place another layer of paper towel on top, then microwave in 30 second bursts until the basil is dry. The basil should feel like dry leaves but still be green. Place the salt and 4 g (⅛ oz) of the basil in a spice or coffee grinder and blitz until you obtain a green powder.

To make the sauce, in a medium saucepan, combine 300 g (10½ oz) of the butter with the lemon juice, salt and water and cook over a medium-high heat until the butter is almost melted. Take it off the heat and add the remaining butter and the grated caciocavallo. Using a hand blender, emulsify everything together – blend until all the butter is completely melted, the cheese is well incorporated and you have a creamy, pale yellow sauce. Keep the sauce in a warm spot.

Boil the gnocchi according to the package instructions. While the gnocchi is cooking, put the sauce in a large frying pan and warm it over a low heat. When the gnocchi are cooked, add them to the sauce and toss through.

TO SERVE Place a burrata in the middle of each plate, sprinkle with pine nuts, spoon over some basil pesto and scatter with basil leaves. Dust the burrata with the basil salt, and serve.

SERVES 4

180 GNOCCHI WITH EGGPLANT, CHILLI, OLIVES & CAPERS

INGREDIENTS

olive oil
1 large eggplant (aubergine), diced
1 batch napoli sauce (see page 177)
200 g (7 oz) breadcrumbs
1 tablespoon kalamata olives, pitted and halved
1 teaspoon baby capers
1 long red chilli, sliced into rounds
400 g (14 oz) gnocchi
¼ bunch flat-leaf (Italian) parsley, finely chopped, to garnish
4 × 90 g (3 oz) burratas
lemon zest, to garnish

METHOD

Warm 2 tablespoons of olive oil in a large frying pan over a medium heat. Once hot, add the diced eggplant and fry for 5 minutes or until golden, stirring occasionally.

Prepare the napoli sauce according to the instructions on page 177.

Combine the breadcrumbs and 20 ml (¾ fl oz) olive oil in a large frying pan. Bring to a medium heat and toss until the breadcrumbs are golden and crispy, then set aside to cool.

TO ASSEMBLE AND PLATE Heat a drizzle of olive oil in a large saucepan over a medium heat. Add the olives, capers and chilli and cook for 1 minute, then add the napoli sauce and continue cooking to heat through. While the sauce is heating up, boil the gnocchi according to the package instructions. When they are cooked, add them to the sauce, toss through and season with salt if necessary. Plate the gnocchi in bowls and garnish with the breadcrumbs, parsley, burrata and lemon zest. Season the burrata with olive oil, salt and black pepper, and serve.

SERVES 5

PACCHERI, 'NDUJA & BURRATA

INGREDIENTS

450 g (1 lb) paccheri
150 g (5½ oz) 'nduja
5 × 90 g (3 oz) burratas
olive oil
20 basil leaves
1 batch napoli sauce (see page 177)

METHOD

Prepare the napoli sauce according to the instructions on page 177.

Bring a large pot of heavily salted water to the boil. Add the paccheri and cook according to the package instructions until al dente. Once cooked, drain the pasta, reserving some of the cooking water.

While the paccheri is cooking, warm up the napoli sauce and add the 'nduja. Mix until you have a smooth sauce, then add the cooked paccheri to the sauce and stir through. If the mixture is looking dry add some of the pasta water. Toss to combine and season to taste.

Serve the pasta on flat plates with a burrata on the side. Season with olive oil and salt, and scatter with basil leaves.

SERVES 3

184 PAPPARDELLE WITH WILD MUSHROOM, PANCETTA & THYME

INGREDIENTS

300 g (10½ oz) pappardelle
150 g (5½ oz) butter
250 g (9 oz) mixed mushrooms (portobello, pine mushroom and king oyster), cleaned and cut into bite-sized pieces
30 g (1 oz) pancetta, diced
1 teaspoon fresh thyme leaves
100 ml (3½ fl oz) white wine
⅓ bunch flat-leaf (Italian) parsley, roughly chopped
3 mini (60 g/2 oz) burratas
olive oil
black pepper

METHOD

Bring a large saucepan of water to the boil, add salt and cook the pappardelle according to the packet instructions until al dente.

While the pasta is cooking, warm a large frying pan over a medium–high heat then add the butter and the mushrooms and pancetta. Cook for around 6–8 minutes until caramelised nicely, then add the thyme and cook for 1 minute. Deglaze with white wine, then add one ladle of the cooking water from the pasta. Add the pasta and toss to mix everything together and create a buttery sauce. Season with salt and black pepper to taste, then sprinkle with parsley. Toss one more time and then serve.

TO SERVE Place the burratas on top and season with olive oil, salt and black pepper.

SERVES 2

SPAGHETTI WITH MUSSELS & FENNEL TOPS

INGREDIENTS

olive oil
½ lemon, cut into 4 pieces
1 onion, sliced
200 ml (7 fl oz) white wine
18 mussels, washed and debearded
2 large red capsicums (bell peppers), julienned
5 basil leaves
15 g (½ oz) butter
200 g (7 oz) spaghetti
1 long red chilli, finely sliced, plus extra to garnish (optional)
2 mini (60 g/2 oz) burratas
black pepper
fennel fronds, to garnish

METHOD

Heat a drizzle of olive oil in a large saucepan with a lid. Add the lemon and half the onion and cook for 2 minutes. Deglaze with the wine then add the mussels. Put the lid on the pan and wait until the mussels are open. When they have opened, sieve the mussels (reserve the cooking liquid) and gently remove the mussel meat from the shells.

Warm a drizzle of olive oil in the pan you used to cook the mussels, then add the capsicums and the remaining onion and cook until softened. Add the basil, then transfer the mixture to a blender along with the butter. Blend, gradually adding some of the cooking liquid from the mussels until you achieve a smooth, silky sauce. (Don't add all the cooking liquid – just enough for flavour and to achieve the right consistency.)

TO SERVE Cook the pasta in a large pot of boiling water according to the package instructions until al dente. When the pasta is almost cooked, heat a drizzle of olive oil in a large pan, then cook the sliced chilli over a low heat for 1 minute. Add the capsicum sauce, the mussels and the pasta, toss, and season to taste. Transfer to plates and add a burrata to each. Season the burrata with salt, pepper and olive oil, add some more chilli (if using) and garnish with fennel fronds.

SERVES 4

188 SPAGHETTI CON PESTO DI PISTACHIO & PRAWN TARTARE

INGREDIENTS

400 g (14 oz) spaghetti
2 mini (60 g/2 oz) burratas, halved
10 g (¼ oz) pistachios, crushed
olive oil

PRAWN TARTARE
4 king prawns, cleaned and finely chopped
olive oil
lime zest

PISTACHIO PESTO
30 g (1 oz) spinach
50 g (1¾ oz) basil leaves
170 g (6 oz) pistachios
250 ml (8½ fl oz) olive oil
1 teaspoon lemon zest
2 teaspoons salt

METHOD

To prepare the prawn tartare, season the prawn meat with salt, olive oil and lime zest.

Next, make the pesto. Blanch the spinach and basil in a large saucepan of boiling water, then refresh in iced water. Pat dry using a tea towel (dish towel). Put the leaves in a blender along with the pistachios, olive oil, lemon zest and salt, then blend until completely smooth.

Cook the pasta in boiling water according to the package instructions until al dente. Warm a large frying pan over a medium heat. Add the pasta, along with a splash of the cooking water, then add the pesto and toss together. It is important to not leave the pasta on the heat for too long, otherwise the pesto will lose its vibrant green colour. Season to taste with salt, and add more pasta water to loosen if needed.

TO SERVE Plate the pasta, then top each plate with half a burrata. Place a quenelle of prawn tartare on top of the burrata, then sprinkle the crushed pistachio over the dish and season the burrata with olive oil and salt.

SERVES 3

TRUFFLE TAGLIATELLE

INGREDIENTS

280 g (10 oz) tagliatelle
3 × 90 g (3 oz) burratas
olive oil
12 g (½ oz) black truffles, very thinly shaved

BEURRE FONDUE

150 ml (5 fl oz) water
1 teaspoon salt
zest of ½ lemon
450 g (1 lb) butter

METHOD

To make the beurre fondue, put the water, salt, lemon zest and three-quarters of the butter in a saucepan over a medium–high heat. When the butter is almost melted, take off the heat and add the rest of the butter. Using a hand blender, emulsify everything together (blend until all the butter is completely melted and you have a creamy sauce – the colour of the sauce should be a pale yellow). Keep the sauce in a warm place or a bain-marie. If the sauce gets cold, it will split.

TO ASSEMBLE AND PLATE Cook the tagliatelle in a large pot of salted boiling water until al dente. When the pasta is about 4 minutes away, put the sauce in a large frying pan over a low heat. Add the pasta and toss to combine. Serve immediately, transferring to plates and topping each plate with a burrata. Season with olive oil, salt and shaved truffle.

SERVES 6

194 VEGETABLE LASAGNE

INGREDIENTS

1 quantity napoli sauce (see page 177)
2 eggplants (aubergines), diced
olive oil
3 brown onions, finely diced
3 red capsicums (bell peppers), deseeded and diced
4 zucchini, diced
1 teaspoon dried oregano
black pepper
2 eggs, beaten
4 lasagne sheets
250 g (9 oz) mozzarella, grated, plus extra for the top
6 × 30 g (1 oz) baby burratas

METHOD

Preheat the oven to 200°C (390°F). Prepare the napoli sauce according to the instructions on page 177.

In a frying pan over a medium heat, fry the eggplant in a little olive oil for 3–5 minutes, until soft, then remove with a slotted spoon and set aside. In the same pan, fry the onions and capsicums for 5 minutes, until soft.

Add the zucchini and fry for another 2–3 minutes. Once the zucchini is soft, return the eggplant to the pan, season well with oregano, salt and pepper and stir until well combined. Turn off the heat and allow to cool. Add the eggs and stir once again to combine.

To assemble the lasagne, layer the bottom of a rectangular baking dish with a few spoonfuls of napoli sauce. Lay one of the lasagne sheets over the top, followed by a few more spoonfuls of napoli sauce, some of the mozzarella, some cooked vegetables and another lasagne sheet. Repeat this process until you have used all the mozzarella (reserving some for the top), vegetables, lasagne sheets and sauce.

Scatter some extra mozzarella over the top and bake in the oven for 15 minutes.

Allow to slightly cool and set before serving.

TO SERVE Cut into six portions and top each piece with a baby burrata.

SERVES 4

196 ORECCHIETTE WITH CIMA DI RAPE & BURRATA

INGREDIENTS

1 kg (2 lb 3 oz) cima di rapa (broccoli rabe)
400 g (14 oz) dried orecchiette
30 ml (1 fl oz) olive oil
3 garlic cloves, finely chopped
3 anchovies, roughly chopped
2 teaspoons red chilli flakes
300 g (10½ oz) Italian sausage, cases removed and roughly chopped
6–8 baby (30 g/1 oz) burratas
handful taralli, crushed, or fried breadcrumbs

METHOD

Bring a pot of salted water to the boil and add the cima di rapa. Cook until slightly tender – about 30 seconds to 1 minute. Remove the cima di rapa with a slotted spoon and set aside.

Add the orecchiette to the same water and cook until al dente. Drain and set aside.

In a large saucepan over a low heat, cook the oil, garlic, anchovies and red chilli flakes for 1–2 minutes, until fragrant.

Add the sausage and fry for 5 minutes, until cooked through and caramelised. Add the cooked orecchiette and the cima di rape to the sauce and toss gently to combine, cooking for another 2–3 minutes. Season with salt to taste and remove from heat.

TO SERVE Plate the pasta and add a baby burrata on top, along with toasted breadcrumbs.

5

SIDES

SERVES 4

RADICCHIO & GREMOLATA INSALATA

INGREDIENTS

100 g (3½ oz) rocket (arugula)
½ radicchio, sliced
2 radishes, thinly sliced
1 quantity lemon dressing (see page 131)
4 × 90 g (3 oz) burratas
30 g (1 oz) toasted walnuts

PICKLED FENNEL

1 large bulb fennel
100 ml (3½ fl oz) water
100 ml (3½ fl oz) white vinegar
1 star anise
3 black peppercorns
70 g (2½ oz) white sugar

GREMOLATA

½ bunch flat-leaf (Italian) parsley, finely chopped
20 g (¾ oz) olive oil
zest of 1 lemon
2 teaspoons lemon juice

METHOD

Prepare the pickled fennel 12 hours before completing the dish. Place all the ingredients except the fennel in a small saucepan. Bring to a boil, then turn off the heat, cover with a lid and let the mixture infuse for another 5 minutes. Strain the liquid.

Meanwhile, thinly slice the fennel. Mix the fennel and pickling liquid in a vacuum pack if possible, otherwise mix in a container, making sure the fennel is completely submerged in the liquid.

Next, prepare the gremolata. Blend or mix all the ingredients together, then set aside.

TO SERVE Drain the pickled fennel and place in a bowl with the rocket, sliced radicchio and radish. Toss through the lemon dressing and season with salt if necessary. Place a burrata in the centre, then add the walnuts. Season the burratas with the gremolata and drizzle some more gremolata around the salad.

SERVES 3

204 MEXICAN BEANS WITH BURRATA

INGREDIENTS

5 yellow corn tortillas
olive oil
3 mini (60 g/2 oz) burratas
5 lemon or lime wedges
1 long red chilli, sliced into rounds
flat-leaf (Italian) parsley, to garnish
black pepper

BRAISED CANNELLINI BEANS

30 g (1 oz) onion, finely sliced
30 g (1 oz) celery, finely sliced
30 g (1 oz) carrot, finely sliced
600 g (1 lb 5 oz) canned cannellini beans, drained and rinsed
15 g (½ oz) tomato paste
35 g (1¼ oz) garam masala
500 g (1 lb 2 oz) canned Italian diced tomatoes
200 ml (7 fl oz) water
80 g (2¾ oz) butter
1 teaspoon white sugar
100 g (3½ oz) spinach

METHOD

To make the beans, heat a drizzle of olive oil in a large saucepan over a medium heat, then add the onion, celery and carrot. Cook for 4 minutes, then add the cannellini beans and cook for a further 2 minutes. Add the tomato paste and garam masala and cook for 3 more minutes, then add the diced tomatoes and the water. Cook over a low heat for 10 minutes, or until the tomatoes start to dissolve, then add the butter, sugar and spinach. Cook for another 2 minutes – by now the mixture should have formed a thick sauce. Season to taste with salt, and add more sugar if needed to balance the acid. Set aside.

Preheat the oven to 180°C (360°F). Cut the tortillas into quarters and arrange them in an oven tray lined with baking paper. Drizzle with olive oil and salt, and then bake for 8 minutes, or until golden and crispy.

TO PLATE Spread the braised beans on a large plate. Top with a burrata, lemon, chilli and parsley, and drizzle the burrata with olive oil, salt and pepper. Serve with the corn chips.

SERVES 3

206 ROASTED PUMPKIN & BROCCOLINI SALAD

INGREDIENTS

3 mini (60 g/2 oz) burratas

ROASTED PUMPKIN

800 g (1 lb 12 oz) pumpkin (winter squash), peeled and cut into chunks
olive oil
black pepper

CRISPY QUINOA

80 g (2¾ oz) quinoa
vegetable oil, for frying

LIME DRESSING

150 ml (5 fl oz) lime juice
1 teaspoon salt
1 tablespoon honey
1 tablespoon dijon mustard
black pepper
150 ml (5 fl oz) olive oil

ROASTED BROCCOLINI

2 bunches broccolini
olive oil
black pepper

METHOD

First, roast the pumpkin. Preheat the oven to 180°C (360°F). Toss the pumpkin in a bowl with salt, olive oil and black pepper, then arrange on a tray lined with baking paper and bake for 30 minutes, or until fully cooked.

Fill a medium saucepan with water and bring to the boil. Add the quinoa and a pinch of salt and simmer for 15 minutes. Drain, and spread the quinoa on a tray lined with baking paper, then refrigerate for a couple of hours to let it dry.

Fill a saucepan with enough oil to deep-fry and bring it to 180°C (360°F). While the oil is heating up, separate the quinoa with your hands so it is as loose as possible. Fry the quinoa, mixing with tongs until the quinoa is golden and crispy. Drain on a plate lined with paper towel and season to taste with salt.

To make the dressing, mix all the ingredients except for the oil in a bowl. Once combined, whisk in the oil slowly to make a dressing.

Return the oven to 180°C (360°F). Next, fill a medium saucepan with salted water and bring to the boil. Blanch the broccolini for 1 minute, then drain and toss in a bowl with olive oil, salt and black pepper.

Transfer to a tray lined with baking paper and bake in the oven for 10 minutes, or until fully cooked.

TO SERVE Arrange the broccolini and the pumpkin on a large plate, then add the burratas. Drizzle everything with the lime dressing and the quinoa, then season the burrata with salt to finish.

SERVES 2

CAPSICUM WITH CRISPY POTATOES & BURRATA

INGREDIENTS

2 mini (60 g/2 oz) burratas
4 chives, cut into 1 cm (½ in) lengths
black pepper

PICKLED CHILLI
1 long red chilli
100 ml (3½ fl oz) white wine vinegar

CRISPY POTATOES
vegetable oil, for frying
1 large chipper potato, skin on

PEPERONATA
185 g (6½ oz) red capsicums (bell peppers), julienned
285 g (10 oz) brown onion, julienned
157 g (5½ oz) cherry tomatoes, halved
45 ml (1½ fl oz) red wine vinegar
60 ml (2 fl oz) olive oil
1½ teaspoons salt
1 teaspoon white sugar

METHOD

To make the pickled chilli, slice the chilli into rounds and put them in a container with the vinegar. Allow to sit for 10–15 minutes before using.

Next, prepare the potatoes. Fill a saucepan with enough oil to deep-fry and bring it to 180°C (360°F). While the oil is heating up, wash and peel the potatoes. Slice the potatoes with a mandolin fitted with the julienne blade. Dry the potatoes and deep-fry in batches (1 cup at a time) until golden brown and crispy. Transfer to a paper towel-lined plate and season.

To make the peperonata, mix all the ingredients in a pot with a lid and bring to the boil. Simmer for 10 minutes, or until the vegetables are fully cooked, mixing from time to time. Set aside and keep warm.

TO SERVE Spoon the peperonata onto a large plate, then arrange the burratas and potatoes around the edge. Garnish with the pickled chilli and the chives, then season the burrata with salt, black pepper and olive oil.

SERVES 4

210 BURRATA WITH SPICY CARROTS & SPATZLE

INGREDIENTS

olive oil
4 × 90 g (3 oz) burratas
16 heirloom carrots
chilli oil, to serve
black pepper
4 chives, cut into 1 cm (½ in) lengths

SPATZLE

160 g (5½ oz) plain (all-purpose) flour
120 g (4½ oz) cornflour (cornstarch)
1 teaspoon salt
1 teaspoon olive oil
330 ml (11 fl oz) water
vegetable oil, for deep-frying

CARROT SAUCE

olive oil
5 large carrots, peeled and cut into half moons
½ brown onion, julienned
4 sprigs thyme
4 black peppercorns
30 ml (1 fl oz) white wine
50 g (1¾ oz) butter

METHOD

Clean the heirloom carrots – there's no need to peel them. Fill a medium saucepan with water and salt heavily. Bring the water to the boil, then blanch the carrots until they are tender but not overcooked – around 2 minutes.

While the carrots are blanching, warm up a grill pan. Once blanched, drain the carrots then arrange them on a tray and drizzle with olive oil. Cook them in the grill pan until you get grill marks, then set aside.

To make the spatzle, mix all the ingredients together until well incorporated, then transfer the mixture to a squeeze bottle.

Fill a large saucepan with enough oil to deep-fry, then heat to 180°C (360°F). Scoop about one-third of the batter into a spatzle maker, or use a spatula and grater and press the batter through the large holes, straight into the oil. Cook the spatzle for approximately 1 minute, or until golden and crunchy. Drain on a plate lined with paper towel, then sprinkle with salt. The spatzle should be very crunchy and light.

Next, make the carrot sauce. Heat a drizzle of olive oil in a large saucepan, then add the carrots, onion, thyme and peppercorns and cook for 6–8 minutes, mixing from time to time until the ingredients are caramelised but not burnt. Deglaze with white wine and let the alcohol evaporate, then add enough water to cover all the ingredients and cook until the carrots are tender. Strain the mixture, reserving the liquid, then transfer the cooked vegetables to a blender with the butter and blitz to obtain a puree. If the puree is too thick, add some of the reserved cooking liquid – the puree should be silky and smooth. Season to taste, then set aside.

TO SERVE Spoon the carrot sauce over a large plate and top with the burratas. Arrange the heirloom carrots and spatzle around the burrata, then season with chilli oil, salt and black pepper and sprinkle with chives.

CAPRESE IN AGRODOLCE

INGREDIENTS

3 slices ciabatta
4 mini (60 g/2 oz) burratas
15 basil leaves
1 quantity basil oil (see page 148)

ROASTED TOMATOES
3 punnets medley heirloom tomatoes
black pepper
olive oil

AGRODOLCE DRESSING
50 ml (1¾ fl oz) olive oil
60 ml (2 fl oz) honey
1 teaspoon salt
120 ml (4 fl oz) red wine vinegar

METHOD

To roast the tomatoes, preheat the oven to 170°C (340°F). Cut the tomatoes in half, place in a bowl and season with salt, black pepper and olive oil. Arrange on a tray lined with baking paper, then roast for 40 minutes to 1 hour, until they are cooked but not mashed.

To make the agrodolce dressing, combine all the ingredients in a small saucepan and bring them to a boil. Remove from the heat and set aside to cool.

Now make the croutons. Increase the oven temperature to 180°C (360°F). Cut the ciabatta into bite-sized pieces, then transfer to a bowl and toss with salt and olive oil. Bake in the oven for 5–8 minutes, giving them a shake from time to time to ensure an even colour.

TO SERVE Spoon the tomatoes onto a large plate, then surround with the burratas, croutons and basil leaves. Season the burratas with basil oil, salt and pepper, then drizzle everything with the agrodolce dressing.

SERVES 1

214 KALE, PECAN & PEAR SALAD

INGREDIENTS

6 kale leaves, cut in chiffonade
½ green pear, cored and slice lengthwise approx. 3 mm (⅛ in) thick
½ red pear, cored and sliced lengthwise approx. 3 mm (⅛ in) thick
1 mini (60 g/2 oz) burrata
black pepper

LIME DRESSING

75 ml (2½ fl oz) lime juice
1 teaspoon salt
1 tablespoon honey
1 teaspoon dijon mustard
black pepper
75 ml (2½ fl oz) olive oil

CANDIED PECANS

2 tablespoons soft brown sugar
1 teaspoon water
¼ teaspoon vanilla extract
50 g (1¾ oz) pecans

METHOD

To make the dressing, mix all the ingredients except for the oil in a bowl. Once combined, whisk in the oil slowly to make a dressing.

Next, prepare the candied pecans. Combine the sugar, water and vanilla extract in a small saucepan and stir over a low heat until the sugar has dissolved. Add the pecans and mix for 3–4 minutes, until the pecans are coated in the caramel. Transfer to a tray lined with baking paper and set aside to cool.

TO SERVE Mix the kale and the lime dressing in a bowl, then arrange the pears and the burrata on top. Season the burrata with salt and pepper, add the candied pecans and drizzle more lime dressing over the pears and the salad.

SERVES 3

216 CITRUS SUMMER SALAD

INGREDIENTS

2 whole grapefruit
¾ radicchio
100 g (3½ oz) rocket (arugula)
black pepper
3 mini (60 g/2 oz) burratas

HONEY AND ROSEMARY DRESSING
2 tablespoons coriander seeds, plus extra for garnish
120 ml (4 fl oz) olive oil
50 g (1¾ oz) honey
3 sprigs rosemary
1½ teaspoons salt
7 teaspoons fresh orange juice
6 teaspoons lemon juice

METHOD

Peel the grapefruit and slice them into rounds using a sharp knife.

To make the honey and rosemary dressing, preheat the oven to 180°C (360°F). Place the coriander seeds in a small tray and toast them in the oven for 4 minutes, then set aside to cool.

Combine the olive oil, honey, rosemary and salt in a small saucepan and bring to the boil over a low heat, stirring until the honey has dissolved. Remove from the heat, add the coriander seeds, then set aside to cool. When the oil is cold, pass it through a sieve to remove the rosemary sprigs and coriander seeds, then add the orange juice and lemon juice to the oil and stir through.

Wash and slice the radicchio, then mix it with the rocket in a bowl. Toss with the honey and rosemary dressing and season to taste.

Place the burratas on top of the salad and arrange the grapefruit segments around it.

Drizzle some fragrant oil on top of the burratas, then sprinkle with salt and the reserved coriander seeds.

SERVES 2

MORA

By Dario di Clerico, Ugo Burrata Bar

INGREDIENTS

500 g (1 lb 2 oz) green beans, trimmed
1 bulb fennel, cut into quarters
50 g (1¾ oz) blackberries, to garnish
2 baby (30 g/1 oz) burratas

BLACKBERRY DRESSING
75 g (2¾ oz) blackberries
50 ml (1¾ fl oz) olive oil
25 ml (¾ fl oz) red wine vinegar
50 ml (1¾ fl oz) water
black pepper

METHOD

Start by making the blackberry dressing. Combine the blackberries, olive oil, red wine vinegar, water and black pepper in a blender and blitz until you get a smooth consistency.

In a medium saucepan, bring some salted water to the boil, then blanch the beans in the boiling water for 5 minutes. Drain and set aside.

TO SERVE Arrange the beans on a plate, scatter the fennel around and top with the burratas. Garnish with blackberries and drizzle the dressing over the top.

SERVES 4

220 PEPERONATA

By Dario di Clerico, Ugo Burrata Bar

INGREDIENTS

olive oil
1 white onion, finely chopped
6 red capsicums (bell peppers), deseeded, stems removed, finely sliced
1 tablespoon red wine vinegar
black pepper
basil leaves, to garnish
4 x 30 g (1 oz) baby burratas
toasted ciabatta, to serve

METHOD

Place a frying pan over medium-low heat, add a drizzle of olive oil and the onion and gently sauté for 5 minutes until softened. Add the sliced capsicums and red wine vinegar, season to taste, stir well and cover. Simmer for 30 minutes on a low heat or until the capsicums are soft and tender.

TO SERVE Spread a layer of peperonata on each plate, topped with a baby burrata. Garnish with basil leaves, drizzle with olive oil and serve with toasted ciabatta.

6

SNACKS

SERVES 2

BURRATA ON TOAST WITH CRISPY BRESAOLA, TOMATOES & PESTO

INGREDIENTS

4 slices of bresaola
250 g (9 oz) medley heirloom tomatoes
black pepper
olive oil
4 slices ciabatta
1 quantity basil pesto (see page 131)
2 × 90 g (3 oz) burratas
1 quantity basil oil (see page 148)
basil leaves

METHOD

Preheat the oven to 180°C (360°F) fan-forced. Place the bresaola on a tray lined with baking paper, then cover with another piece of baking paper, and sit another tray on top. Bake for 10 minutes, or until the bresaola is completely crispy, then transfer to a piece of paper towel to drain the excess oil.

Halve or quarter the tomatoes and transfer them to a bowl. Season with salt, black pepper and olive oil, then set aside.

In a griddle pan, toast the sliced ciabatta bread for about 2 minutes on each side or until golden.

TO SERVE Arrange the toasted ciabatta on a plate, then spoon some basil pesto over the top. Place the burratas on the toast and scatter the tomatoes all around. Season the burrata with basil oil and salt, then finally, scatter the basil leaves and crispy bresaola all around the dish.

SERVES 1

228 FRIED BURRATA

INGREDIENTS

1 tablespoon balsamic glaze
5 slices mortadella
2 tablespoons pistachios, crushed in a food processor
black pepper
basil leaves, to garnish

CRUMBED BURRATA

1 × 90 (3 oz) burrata
100 g (3½ oz) plain (all-purpose) flour
100 g (3½ oz) breadcrumbs
2 eggs + a splash of milk, for egg wash
vegetable oil, for deep-frying

METHOD

To make the crumbed burrata, prepare three separate bowls, one with flour, one with egg wash and one with breadcrumbs. Drain the burrata, then gently roll it in the flour, then dip it in the egg wash and finish with the breadcrumbs.

To deep-fry, fill a small saucepan with enough oil to submerge the burrata completely. Bring the oil to 180°C (360°F) and fry the burrata for around 2 minutes, or until golden and crispy. Drain on a plate lined with paper towel, then season with salt and black pepper.

TO SERVE Drizzle a plate with the balsamic glaze, then layer the mortadella to create a bed for the burrata. Place the burrata on top, sprinkle with crushed pistachios and garnish with basil leaves.

SERVES 1

230 BAGUETTE WITH BRESAOLA, ROCKET & SHAVED GRANA

INGREDIENTS

1 sourdough baguette
10 g (¼ oz) Grana Padano
20 g (¾ oz) rocket (arugula)
olive oil
7 thin slices bresaola
1 × 90 g (3 oz) burrata
black pepper

METHOD

Slice the baguette in half, then set aside. Using a peeler, shave the Grana Padano and add it to a mixing bowl. Add the rocket and season with olive oil and salt.

TO ASSEMBLE Place the salad in the baguette, then top with the bresaola and add the burrata. Season with olive oil, salt and black pepper. Alternatively, you can also try these delicious combinations:

- Smoked salmon, rocket and burrata
- Pesto, mortadella and burrata
- Prosciutto, burrata and avocado

SERVES 1

232 PANINO WITH 'NDUJA & BURRATA

INGREDIENTS

20 g (¾ oz) salad mix
black pepper
olive oil
1 heirloom tomato, thinly sliced
1 ciabatta roll
15 g (½ oz) 'nduja
1 × 90 g (3 oz) burrata

METHOD

In a bowl, mix the salad with salt, black pepper and olive oil, then set aside. Toss the tomato slices in a bowl with salt, pepper and olive oil.

Cut the roll in half and spread the 'nduja over the base. (Note, 'nduja should be easy to spread, like soft butter. If your 'nduja is very hard, add some olive oil and mix until you have a smooth texture.)

Top the 'nduja with the salad mix and the tomato, and then the burrata. Season with salt, pepper and olive oil, and serve.

WHAT IS 'NDUJA?

Pronounced 'en-doo-ya', 'nduja is a spicy, spreadable pork sausage that stems from the Southern region of Calabria in Italy.

It is made from pork, fat, herbs and Calabrian chilli peppers, which gives it its fiery taste. 'Nduja is normally served with slices of bread along with cheese, but over the years, it has become quite a versatile ingredient as it can be added to many dishes.

Add this unique ingredient to your pasta dishes, soups and stews or spread on top of pizza.

SERVES 1

PANINO WITH MORTADELLA, PESTO & BURRATA

INGREDIENTS

1 ciabatta roll
1 tablespoon basil pesto (see page 131)
4 slices mortadella
1 × 125 g (4½ oz) burrata
black pepper
olive oil

METHOD

Slice the roll in half, then spread the pesto over the base. Top with the mortadella then the burrata, and season with salt, black pepper and olive oil.

WHAT IS MORTADELLA?

Mortadella originated in the Northern region of Italy in Bologna.

Mortadella is made from pork, beef fat and pork fat, which is seasoned with pepper and then slowly cooked for 24 hours. Once cooked and cooled, it is then sliced thinly into sheets.

The cured meat is traditionally served inside a panini, on a pizza, with giardiniera and on cheese boards.

SERVES 1

236 THE UGO

By Dario di Clerico, Ugo Burrata Bar

INGREDIENTS

1 × 3 kg (6 lb 10 oz) piece porchetta
rosemary leaves
black pepper
focaccia bread
1 × 125 g (4½ oz) burrata

SALSA VERDE

1 bunch flat-leaf (Italian) parsley
1 bunch basil, leaves picked
1 boiled egg
2 slices bread, coated in vinegar
150 ml (5 fl oz) olive oil

METHOD

To make the salsa verde, combine all the ingredients in a blender and blitz until smooth.

Butterfly the porchetta and lay it on your work surface skin side down. Season well with rosemary leaves, salt and black pepper. Roll up and secure with baking twine. Pat the skin dry and allow to rest, uncovered, in the fridge overnight. You want to remove as much moisture as possible, as this will allow the crackle to crisp up when cooking.

Preheat the oven to 200°C (390°F) and line a baking tray with baking paper. Put the porchetta on the lined tray and bake for 1 hour, then reduce the heat to 100°C (210°F) and cook for a further 1 hour, until the centre of the porchetta reaches 70°C (160°F). Remove the twine and allow the porchetta to rest before slicing.

TO ASSEMBLE Slice the focaccia in half and add a few spoonfuls of salsa verde to the base. Add two slices of porchetta, then top with the burrata. Slice open the burrata with a knife, allowing the cheese to completely cover the porchetta. Season with a little salt and pepper and cover with the other half of the focaccia.

7

SWEETS

SERVES 1

BURRATA WITH RUM BABA

by Dario di Clerico, Ugo Burrata Bar

INGREDIENTS

1 × 60 g (2 oz) burrata
shaved macadamias, to serve

RUM BABA

2½ teaspoons dried yeast
125 ml (4 fl oz) warm milk
2½ tablespoons white sugar
485 g (1 lb 1 oz) plain (all-purpose) flour, plus extra for dusting
½ teaspoon salt
4 eggs, whisked
melted butter, for greasing
180 g (6½ oz) unsalted butter, cubed and softened

SYRUP

330 g (11½ oz) white sugar
200 ml (7 fl oz) cold water
180 ml (6 fl oz) dark rum

METHOD

To make the rum babas, in a bowl, combine the yeast with half of the warm milk and ½ teaspoon of the sugar. Let it sit in a warm place for 10 minutes, or until the mixture becomes frothy.

While the yeast is activating, sift the flour and salt into a large bowl. Create a well in the centre, then pour in the yeast mixture, along with the whisked eggs and the remaining milk. Stir gently until a soft, sticky dough forms.

Lightly grease a large bowl with melted butter. Transfer the dough onto a lightly floured surface and knead for about 10 minutes, or until smooth.

Grease a 12-cup bundt pan with melted butter and dust it with flour, shaking off any excess.

Place the dough on a clean work surface and gradually knead in the softened butter. Continue kneading until the dough is smooth and elastic. Shape it into a disc, then create a small hole in the centre with your fingers. Place the dough in the prepared bundt pan. Cover with plastic wrap and let it rise in a warm place for 1 hour, or until the dough reaches the top of the pan.

Preheat the oven to 200°C (390°F). Bake the dough for 10 minutes, then reduce the temperature to 180°C (360°F) and continue baking for an additional 25 minutes, or until a skewer inserted into the centre comes out clean. Remove from the oven and let the cake cool for 5 minutes.

To make the syrup, combine the sugar and water in a saucepan. Cook, stirring, over a medium heat for 2–3 minutes, until the sugar dissolves. Bring the mixture to a gentle boil and allow it to simmer without stirring for about 3 minutes, or until the syrup thickens slightly. Remove from the heat and stir in the rum.

TO SERVE Crumble one baba into the base of a bowl. Add the burrata to the centre of the bowl, then add a generous amount of shaved macadamias and drizzle the rum syrup over the top.

244 POACHED RHUBARB, ORANGE & CAMPARI DRESSING

INGREDIENTS

4 × 125 g (4½ oz) burrata
9–12 navel orange segments
handful rocket (arugula)
orange zest, to garnish

RED CORAL TUILES

90 ml (3 fl oz) water
30 ml (1 fl oz) vegetable oil
1 tablespoon plain (all-purpose) flour
2 g (1⁄16 oz) white sugar
3 drops red food colouring

RHUBARB PUREE & POACHED RHUBARB

400 g (14 oz) white sugar
400 ml (13½ fl oz) water
2 star anise
3 strips orange peel, pith removed
1 bunch rhubarb, cut into 4–5 cm (1½–2 in) lengths

CAMPARI DRESSING

2 tablespoons Campari
1 tablespoon orange juice
1 teaspoon lemon juice
1 teaspoon cooking liquid from rhubarb puree
100 ml (3½ fl oz) olive oil

METHOD

To make the red coral tuiles, mix all the ingredients in a bowl and whisk to combine until the mixture forms a liquid paste. Transfer the mixture to a squeeze bottle. Warm a small non-stick pan over a low–medium heat, then add just enough mix to the pan to make a thin layer. Cook until you start to see a coral-like texture form. Using an offset spatula, carefully transfer the tuile to a plate lined with paper towel to drain the excess oil, then set aside to cool at room temperature. Continue making the tuiles one at a time until all the mixture has been used.

To prepare the rhubarb, preheat the oven to 180°C (360°F). Combine the sugar, water, star anise and orange peel in an ovenproof saucepan and bring to the boil, then add the rhubarb, cover with foil and place in the oven for 5 minutes, or until the rhubarb is cooked (it should hold its structure). Be careful, the rhubarb can overcook very quickly.

Take eight pieces of rhubarb and set them aside, then return the rest to the oven for 5 minutes, or until they are completely soft. Pass the mixture through a sieve, reserving the liquid and discarding the star anise. Put the rhubarb in a blender and blitz until you obtain a silky puree – add some of the reserved cooking liquid if necessary. Set aside to cool, and save some of the cooking liquid for the Campari dressing.

To make the Campari dressing, combine all the ingredients in a blender and blend until smooth.

TO SERVE Spread some of the rhubarb puree over a large plate, then top with the burratas, the poached rhubarb sticks, orange segments, tuile and rocket. To finish, drizzle with the dressing and garnish with orange zest.

SERVES 3

SWEET RICOTTA, POACHED APRICOTS & BURRATA

INGREDIENTS

3 slices bread
3 mini (60 g/2 oz) burratas
almond flakes, lightly toasted, to garnish
mint leaves, to garnish
lime zest, to garnish

SWEET RICOTTA

500 g (1 lb 2 oz) ricotta
25 g (1 oz) caster (superfine) sugar
½ tablespoon olive oil

APRICOTS IN MUSCAT

185 ml (6 fl oz) muscat
80 ml (2½ fl oz) water
75 g (2¾ oz) white sugar
½ vanilla bean, cut in half and seeds scraped (use the pod and the seeds)
5 apricots, cut in half, stones removed

METHOD

To make the sweet ricotta, mix all the ingredients in a blender and puree until smooth.

Next, prepare the apricots in muscat. Combine the muscat, water, sugar and vanilla in a small saucepan and bring it to the boil. Add the apricots, simmer for 2 minutes, then remove from the heat and let the apricots cool down in the liquid.

TO SERVE Toast the bread, then spread each slice with sweet ricotta. Place a burrata in the centre of each slice, then arrange the apricots around the burrata and drizzle with some of the cooking liquid. Sprinkle with almond flakes, mint leaves and lime zest to finish.

SERVES 4

248 BURRATA WITH STRAWBERRIES & WHITE CHOCOLATE

INGREDIENTS

12 strawberries, cut into slices or chunks
35 g (1¼ oz) white chocolate buttons
4 × 90 g (3 oz) burratas
1 tablespoon crushed pistachios
basil leaves, to garnish
1 quantity red coral tuiles (see page 244)

STRAWBERRY PUREE
300 g (10½ oz) frozen strawberries
70 g (2½ oz) caster (superfine) sugar

METHOD

To make the strawberry puree, mix the strawberries and sugar in a medium saucepan and cook, stirring, over a medium–high heat until the sugar is dissolved. Set the mixture aside to cool down in the pan or in another heatproof container. When cold, strain the mixture, reserving the liquid. Put the strawberries in a blender and blitz, gradually adding the cooking liquid until you obtain a thick sauce. Refrigerate until ready to use.

Bitz the white chocolate buttons in a blender or food processor until the mixture forms small chocolate pearls. Note, it is important that the chocolate is cold when you blend it.

TO SERVE Spoon the strawberry puree over each plate, then place a burrata on top. Arrange the cut strawberries around the burrata, sprinkle the white chocolate and pistachios over the top, then scatter with basil leaves and top with a tuile to garnish.

MAKES 4

250 SMORE

by Dario di Clerico, Ugo Burrata Bar

INGREDIENTS

8 digestive or round biscuits
150 g (5½ oz) milk chocolate, chopped
4 × 60 g (2 oz) burratas
100 g (3½ oz) soft brown sugar

METHOD

Preheat the oven to 160°C (320°F). Arrange the biscuits and chocolate on a lined baking tray and warm in the oven for 2–3 minutes, until the chocolate is slightly melted. Remove from the oven and set aside.

Dip the burratas in the brown sugar, then apply a blowtorch for a few minutes, until the sugar starts to caramelise.

TO ASSEMBLE Place each burrata in the centre of a biscuit, then cover with another biscuit and enjoy.

del Latte
€ 23.90

THE STORY OF CHEESE IS ONE OF CONSTANT EVOLUTION

With artisanal practices meeting new technologies and global palates expanding, the future of cheese promises even more diversity and creativity. Sustainability and ethical sourcing are guiding the cheese industry towards more responsible production methods that respect the earth and the welfare of animals. And as consumers become more informed, there's a growing appreciation for cheeses that tell a story of place, tradition and craftsmanship.

A renewed interest in ancient cheesemaking techniques, coupled with the adventurous spirit of modern cheesemakers, points to a vibrant future where past traditions and present innovations coexist harmoniously. With the exploration of lesser-known cheeses, the revival of regional specialties and the global exchange of culinary ideas, the cheese board of tomorrow will be as rich and varied as ever.

Whether you're a seasoned cheese connoisseur or a curious novice, the cheese world offers endless opportunities for discovery. Start locally, exploring the cheeses of your region, then gradually expand your horizons. Attend cheese tastings and cheesemaking demonstrations, visit farms and dairies, and don't hesitate to ask questions. Each cheese you encounter has a story to tell, from the grass that fed the cows to the hands that shaped the finished product.

Experiment in your kitchen, pairing cheeses with unexpected ingredients, cooking traditional recipes, or even attempting to make your own. Share your discoveries with friends and family, spreading the joy and communal spirit that cheese naturally fosters.

Above all, approach each cheese with an open mind. Let your senses guide you, and find joy in the flavour, texture and aromatic nuances. Your cheese journey is not just about tasting different cheeses; it's about connecting with centuries-old traditions, engaging with communities around the globe, and discovering the artistry in every bite.

INDEX

SPECIAL MENTIONS

GRAZIE

I still can't believe that this burrata book, which has been a dream of mine for the past four years, has come to life so wonderfully.

Creating this book has been a labour of passion and love, and it wouldn't have been possible without the support, inspiration and contributions of so many amazing people. I am truly grateful.

A very special thank you goes to my wonderful team at That's Amore Cheese, in particular Serena Zen and Caroline De Luca who contributed in so many ways to this project and really made it possible. In particular a big thank you to our incredible Chef Carlos Naspiran for creating and collecting over sixty recipes that use burrata. Your passion and creativity have created these delicious recipes.

To Dario Di Clerico and Salim Gafayri for their guest recipe contributions to this book, which really add another layer of recipe applications.

To all the producers in Puglia, Italy that have spared their time in sharing so much valuable information for this book, highlighting their incredible passion for this product: Le Delizie del Latte, Caseificio Europa, Caseificio Maldera, Azienda Agricola Querceta and Massari Mozzarella Bar.

To Antonio Asselta and his wife Grazia, who spent two days opening their home to us, introducing us to family members and sharing their incredible multi-generational family history, all the way back to 1928.

To all our dairy farmers and in particular Kerrie, Rob and Holly from Kingsville Jersey Farm, thank you for all your hard work to produce our milk and most importantly for sharing your endless passion for the Jersey cows that you truly care so much for.

A huge thank you to photographer Bonnie Savage for not only capturing the essence of our burrata recipes, Australian milk farms and Italian landscapes through her stunning photography, but for being so involved and passionate about this project well beyond the photography aspect.

To our food stylist, Lisa La Barbera, for her exceptional food styling and creativity, bringing these beautiful burrata dishes to life.

Thank you to Dominique Ho from Viewpoint Digital Media, for writing a story on the creation of burrata and how it has evolved and developed over the years.

Thank you to our wonderful publisher, Hardie Grant and book designer Eloise at Evi-O.Studio for allowing this passion project to come to light over the last few months. To Courtney and her team, thank you for believing in this dream and helping it become a reality for us to share it with the world.

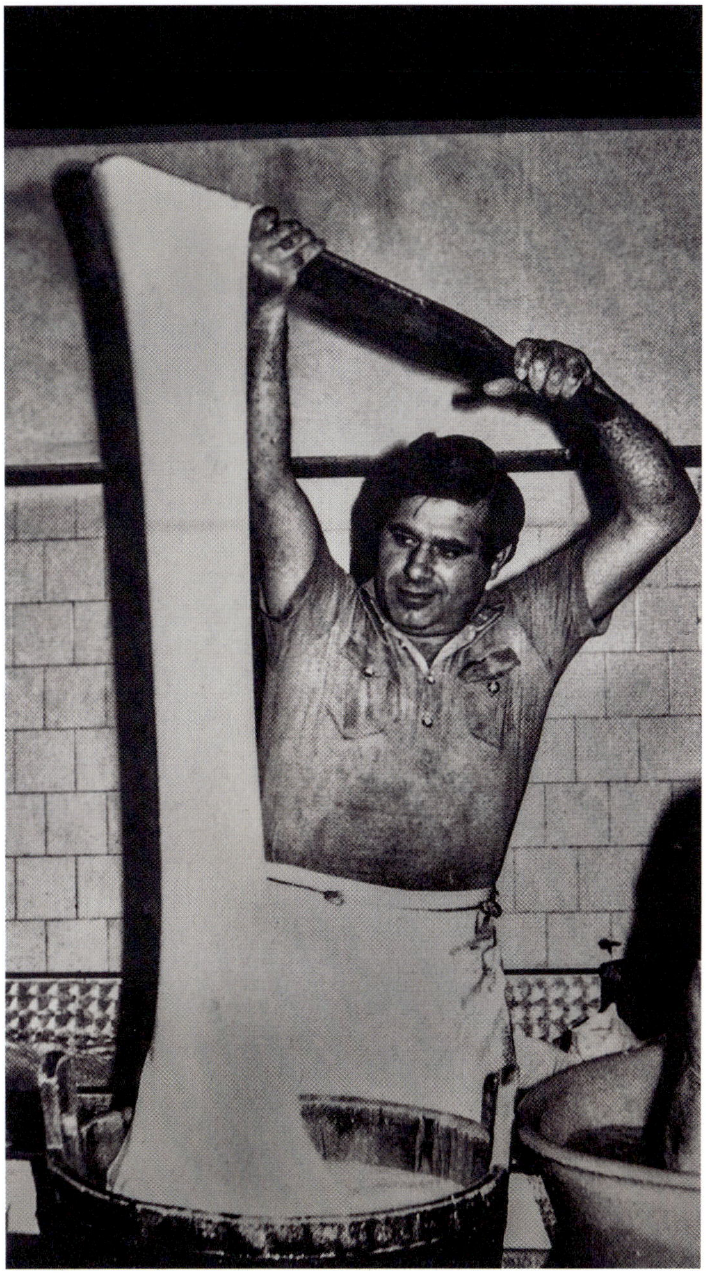

Family photos of Aruanno and Asselta families, past generations of cheesemakers in Andria

FROM LEFT Antonio Asselta, Michele Asselta, Riccardo Asselta, Vincenzo Campamile, Emanuelle Aruanno

Published in 2025 by Hardie Grant Custom
an imprint of Hardie Grant Publishing

Hardie Grant Custom (Melbourne)
Ground Floor, Building 1, 658 Church Street
Richmond VIC 3121, Australia

www.hardiegrant.com.au

Hardie Grant acknowledges the Traditional Owners of the Country on which we work, the Wurundjeri People of the Kulin Nation and the Gadigal People of the Eora Nation, and recognises their continuing connection to the land, waters and culture. We pay our respects to their Elders past and present.

A catalogue record of this book is available from the National Library of Australia.

Burrata
ISBN 9781761451843

FSC www.fsc.org MIX Paper | Supporting responsible forestry FSC® C020056

Publication commissioned by
Courtney Nicholls

Publication managed by
Shahirah Hambali and Mahalia Brooks

Edited by Vanessa Lanaway

Designed by Evi-O.Studio | Eloise Myatt

Photography by Bonnie Savage

Food Styling by Lisa La Barbera

Colour reproduction by
Splitting Image Colour Studio

Printed in China by Leo Paper Group

"A heartfelt thank you to Serena Zen for embracing this idea and bringing this book to life."

– Giorgio Linguanti